WORKING IN JAPAN

Other How To Books on Living & Working Abroad

Applying for a United States Visa
Become an Au Pair
Do Voluntary Work Abroad
Emigrate
Finding a Job in Canada
Finding Work Overseas
Find Temporary Work Abroad
Get a Job Abroad
Get a Job in America
Get a Job in Australia
Get a Job in Europe
Get a Job in France
Get a Job in Germany
Get a Job in Hotels & Catering
Get a Job in Travel & Tourism
Live & Work in America
Live & Work in Australia
Live & Work in France
Live & Work in Germany
Live & Work in the Gulf
Live & Work in Hong Kong
Live & Work in Italy
Live & Work in Japan
Live & Work in New Zealand

Live & Work in Portugal
Live & Work in Saudi Arabia
Live & Work in Spain
Living & Working in Britain
Living & Working in Canada
Living & Working in China
Living & Working in the
Netherlands
Master Languages
Obtaining Visas & Work Permits
Rent & Buy Property in France
Rent & Buy Property in Italy
Retire Abroad
Selling into Japan
Setting Up Home in Florida
Spend a Year Abroad
Study Abroad
Teach Abroad
Travel Round the World
Working Abroad
Working on Contract Worldwide
Working on Cruise Ships
Working in the Gulf
Working as a Holiday Rep
Your Own Business in Europe

Other titles in preparation

The How To series now contains more than 150 titles in the following categories:

Business Matters
Family Reference
Jobs & Careers
Living & Working Abroad
Student Handbooks
Successful Writing

Please send for a free copy of the latest catalogue for full details (see back cover for address).

LIVING & WORKING ABROAD

WORKING IN
JAPAN

How and where to find well paid jobs
in every sector

Jonathan Hayter

How To Books

British Library Cataloguing-in-Publication data
A catalogue record for this book is available from the British Library.

First published 1996 by How To Books Ltd, Plymbridge House, Estover Road, Plymouth PL6 7PZ, United Kingdom. Tel: (01752) 202301. Fax: (01752) 202331.

Note: The material contained in this book is set out in good faith for general guidance and no liability can be accepted for loss or expense incurred as a result of relying in particular circumstances on statements made in the book. The law and regulations are complex and liable to change, and readers should check the current position with the relevant authorities before making personal arrangements.

Produced for How To Books by Deer Park Productions.

Typeset by The Baskerville Press, Salisbury, Wiltshire.
Printed and bound by Cromwell Press, Broughton Gifford, Melksham, Wiltshire.

Contents

List of Illustrations

Preface

The phoenix-like rise of Japan from the ashes of the Second World War to powerhouse economy has been well documented. Very little, however, has been written about the recent emergence of Japan as a major destination for job-seekers. There was a time when the only way a foreigner could make a living, albeit a good one, in Japan was by teaching English. The good news is that those days are gone, even though English teaching does remain an attractive option both for professional teachers and young people newly graduated and wishing to spend a year or two living in Japan. The growing numbers of foreigners resident in Japan speak for themselves. In 1980, fewer than 60,000 Westerners, (USA, UK, Australia, NZ, Canada and the EU) resided in Japan. By 1992, the figure had almost doubled. The kinds of work available to the foreign job-seeker in Japan now range from positions in banking and finance to work as coaches in golf and tennis clubs and at ski resorts. The numbers of foreigners seeking job opportunities in Japan are still small in comparison with countries such as the USA, yet ironically the job potential in Japan is probably greater than in America or any of the member states of the EU. For the time being at least, demand in Japan outweighs supply, meaning you will find yourself in a seller's market. But this won't last for ever. If you are thinking of making that job-seeking trip to Japan, the time is now. Japan boasts the world's second largest economy after the USA. Seven of the world's largest banks are Japanese and so are a considerable percentage of the world's top 500 companies. Manufacturing and service sectors are highly diversified. Japan's high rate of industrial growth in the last three decades was fuelled to a great extent by exports and even today it is Japan's foreign markets that continue to sustain expansion. This 'export or die' mentality of Japanese industry is a phenomenon that has created a wealth of opportunities for foreigners in many fields.

At the time of writing, Japan, like most other industrialised economies, is undergoing a recession. The figures for unemployment, (UK 7 per cent, USA 5.5 per cent, Japan 2 per cent) indicate that the downturn in Japan has not been as damaging as those suffered by the Western economies. All the indications are that the Japanese economic cycle will turn up again in the near future.

Looking further ahead, the technological lead that the country enjoys over its competitors, its highly educated work force and the well-developed work ethic of its people, should see the Japanese economy go from strength to strength in the years to come. Add the rapid development of Japan's major cities into international centres of business and culture, and the numbers of foreigners finding work in Japan can only increase.

By using this book, you will be able to decide whether you possess the kinds of skills that can be marketed in Japan and just as important, whether or not Japan is the kind of place where you would be happy to be based. I am quite sure that if you make the decision to go, it will turn out to be one of the best choices you will ever make, not only in terms of career prospects but also as an opportunity to live and work within one of the world's most fascinating cultures.

I would like to take this opportunity of thanking Mrs Keiko Omizo for her co-operation in producing this book.

Jonathan Hayter

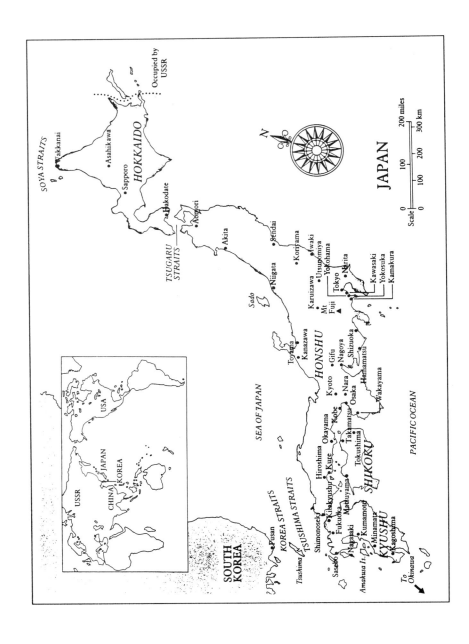

Fig. 1. Map of Japan and major cities.

1
Introduction to
Working in Japan

SEEING THE JOB POTENTIAL IN JAPAN

Japan seems a very long way away from the UK, not only physically but
also in terms of its culture, people, customs and language. Everything
appears alien, everything a part of an essentially inscrutable nation of the
Orient. There will be few people who have not heard something of Japan's
barriers to imports, of the difficulties of living and doing business there.
The likelihood of you possessing the sort of qualities, experience and
character that could find you a job there might seem slim to say the least.
A large and growing number of your fellow countrymen would be very
happy for you to continue to think about Japan in these terms. They are
the people who have gone there and found themselves in a very lucrative
market with many more opportunities for their skills than they could find
in their own country. These people are understandably anxious to keep a
tight lid on competition.

The reality is that Japan is now no more than twelve hours away by air
from the UK. Alongside an ancient culture and traditions, much of life in
Japan has been considerably influenced by the West. As a modern,
industrialised state, you will find many similarities with life in the UK.
Best of all, most of the differences you encounter with life back home will
be positive ones. As for work, the opportunities in Japan are now as
diverse as, if not greater than, you could find in the USA or any EU
member state. Finding a job in Japan, living and working there, is
undoubtedly a challenge, but the rewards of making the effort are
considerable.

Considering the benefits of a job in Japan:

- high salary levels
- high standard of living
- opportunity to develop new skills
- opportunity to gain valuable experience
- opportunity to learn a language that is much in demand
- very low crime rates/little public disorder

- opportunity to live in a fascinating society.

The international Japanese economy:

- is the world's second largest economy
- is the economic centre of East Asia
- offers high standards of living
- experiences high and increasing demand for foreign expertise.

The Japanese economy is founded on the twin pillars of a large internal market of over 120 million consumers together with dominant shares in export markets for consumer electronics, motor vehicles and more recently, banking and financial services. Japan exports worldwide. This creates a demand for English language speakers, not only as teachers but also as managers and for a variety of other roles in Japanese enterprises including:

- English teachers
- English-speaking managers
- lawyers
- accountants
- copywriters
- proofreaders
- translators.

The growing strength of the yen and continuing pressure from foreign governments, or *gai-atsu,* means that Japan is now poised to become a major importer of foreign goods. This huge two-way trade in goods and services will continue to fuel the demand for foreign expertise and know how in fields such as:

- managers and other professional staff for foreign companies operating in Japan

- service personnel for foreign goods sold in Japan

- sales people

- secretaries, receptionists.

Japan's fascination with the West
Japan was closed to outside influences for four hundred years. As a result, the Japanese now have a intense curiosity in the world outside, particularly

in those countries which filled the much respected role of teacher to Japan when the nation undertook its journey to industrialisation. Many Japanese still look with envy at the style of life in Western Europe and the USA. This fascination with the West is reflected in the growing demand for Western goods and services and shows no signs of diminishing. It also creates opportunities for foreigners to work as, amongst other things:

- entertainers
- hostesses
- models
- designers
- hair stylists/beauty therapists
- Western cooks
- travel consultants.

Learning from foreigners

The Japanese place great emphasis on education and learning. Self improvement is a cradle to the grave pursuit, starting at the age of three or four in kindergarten and never really finishing, even after retirement. Consequently, there is a constant and often unfulfilled demand for foreign expertise both to provide education services for individuals and for Japanese business:

- teachers (not only of English but also subjects as diverse as dancing and cooking)

- university/college lecturers

- sports coaches

- consultants for business practices and management techniques

- aerobics/fitness trainers.

BUT IS THERE A JOB IN JAPAN FOR ME?

A wide variety of jobs are available but your success in securing employment in Japan will depend on a number of factors.

Your qualifications

You will find that most jobs in Japan (with some notable exceptions), require the applicant to possess at least a university or polytechnic degree. Depending on the job you are looking for, you may also be required to provide further specialist certificates.

Your experience

Japanese employers place great reliance on experience. You are unlikely to succeed in getting placed in a position of any responsibility without it. Conversely, for many junior positions, the Japanese prefer to employ those without previous experience so that they can start, figuratively speaking, with a clean slate.

Speaking the language

As is the way in any other country, your ability to speak the language is an advantage. But apart from specialist occupations such as translating, you should view speaking Japanese as something that is desirable rather than obligatory from the outset. Clearly though, learning a language that is much in demand is something that anyone working in Japan for any length of time should try to achieve.

Character and temperament

The Japanese value honesty, modesty and an even temper. These are the personal qualities a Japanese employer will be looking for in you. You may be successful in finding a job without these qualities. Whether you will be accepted and succeed in your new position is another matter. Whatever your reason for going to Japan, whether it be simply to earn money, or to take advantage of the opportunities for learning new skills, you will have a hard time unless you actually enjoy your stay. It is important that you be aware of the kind of personal qualities you may need to get along in Japan. Be honest with yourself, and if you feel that you do not possess many or most of these qualities, think very hard before you commit yourself.

Ask yourself whether you are:

- open-minded
- patient
- flexible
- balanced
- diplomatic
- tolerant of manners and attitudes different from your own.

DECIDING WHETHER JAPAN IS THE RIGHT PLACE FOR YOU

Japan and the Japanese do not suit everyone. You should consider carefully, before making your decision to seek a position in Japan, whether you can not only cope with but also positively thrive in the new environment in which you will find yourself.

Minority status

As a Western resident in Japan, you will be a member of a minority group, perhaps for the first time in your life. Being conspicuous can be a claustrophobic experience for some newcomers. Like people the world over, the Japanese, rightly or wrongly, have their own preconceptions as to the nature and behaviour of foreign people. The Japanese are well known for their kindness and hospitality to foreigners, and most of the prejudicial treatment you will receive as a foreigner will be wholly positive. But you should be aware that there may be rare occasions when the reaction of certain Japanese to you as a foreigner is less pleasant.

The cost of living

A few words need to be said about Japan's status as one of the world's most expensive countries. Compared to rates of remuneration in the UK and USA, Japanese salaries appear extremely attractive. You should bear in mind, however, that the cost of living in Japan, especially in the major cities (where you are most likely to find your job), is correspondingly high. Japan is not a place where you can live on the cheap. Having said that, the cost of living in relation to salary levels is certainly no higher than most Western countries and most foreign residents are pleasantly surprised to find that it is no more difficult, if not easier, to live better in Tokyo or Osaka than it is in London, New York or Melbourne.

The language

Japanese is not an easy language to learn, but neither is it an impenetrable puzzle as some commentators have described it. In fact, you can get by in the country with not much more than a basic grounding. However, to get the most out of your stay, both in terms of personal fulfilment and your future career prospects, you should make developing your command of Japanese one of your priorities. Ask yourself whether this is a challenge you are willing to take on.

The work environment

The Japanese work hard and play hard. Not only that, but for the majority of Japanese, loyalty to the company is put before everything else; on occasions, even family. In many Japanese companies, this same dedication is expected of everyone, Japanese and foreigner alike.

Competition in the Japanese economy is fierce and consequently, work can be very demanding at times. This presents a great opportunity to develop experience and skills in a very different environment from the one you are used to. Ask yourself whether this is an opportunity you are ready to take.

Population density
Roughly 10 per cent of the land mass of Japan supports a population of 120 million Japanese, or approximately twice that of the UK. On the other hand, the populations of the Netherlands and Belgium are denser than the population of Japan. You are most likely to find yourself working Toyko, Osaka or one of the other major cities of Japan, alongside the Japanese population. These major conurbations are chronically over-crowded and no place for a claustrophobic, but most foreigners find that they acclimatise to the relative lack of space in a short time. Also, there is a great deal of unspoilt, albeit mountainous, countryside to enjoy in your free time, if you find yourself needing to get away from time to time, and Japan's excellent public transport system makes getting away from the city simple and rapid. Realistically though, the vast majority of the jobs available are to be found in the cities. If you are the sort of person who feels uncomfortable living in a crowded city, you should think long and hard before committing yourself to a job in Japan.

The climate
The Japanese pride themselves on living in a country which, they say, has four distinct seasons. Winters in the north are long and quite severe with four or five months of snow being quite normal. That is great if you like snow and winter sports, very grim if you do not. Summer in central and southern Japan is very hot and excessively humid, particularly during July and August. Late May and June is the time of the annual rainy season, or *tsuyu,* six weeks of oppressively wet, stifling weather. Nobody, least of all the Japanese, claim to enjoy the *tsuyu,* but most people acclimatise after one summer and just learn to accept it as being one of the few disadvantages of living in Japan.

Discrimination against foreigners
Japan was closed to all foreign influence for almost four hundred years during the time of the Tokugawa shogunate and the number of foreigners resident in the country is still low by international standards. It is therefore to be expected that the Japanese still tend to think of themselves as a race apart and look upon foreigners, or *gaigin,* living in their country, as different from themselves and in some cases, undesirable. This may

manifest itself in instances such as a Japanese real estate agent turning away a foreigner looking for an apartment merely because he or she is a foreigner.

Japanese society is very much built upon hierarchies and this rigidity manifests itself in the way the Japanese conceive of foreigners along racial and ethnic lines. The white European or North American is seen as an equal and occasionally a superior, whereas people from the countries of Asia, most notably those that have a history of being colonised by Japan, are looked upon as inferiors. Africans are also widely considered as occupying a position below that of the Japanese.

At the same time, however, the hospitality the Japanese show to visitors to their country is legendary. For every case of negative discrimination you will hear, there will be ten or more stories of the kindness and generosity shown to foreigners by the Japanese. Negative discrimination exists, and when you run into it, it can be frustrating at best, embittering at worst. Taken on balance, however, as a foreigner living in Japan, you are far more likely to be a 'victim' of the positive side of Japanese discrimination than the negative.

The Japanese themselves
Some people who have lived in Japan have nothing but good to say about their hosts. Others view the Japanese less favourably. More than anything else, your own thoughts and feelings about the Japanese will depend upon your own character and about what you look for in other people.

Making generalisations about an ethnic or national group can only ever provide a rough approximation of character, but nevertheless the Japanese as a group can be considered to be the following:

- honest
- industrious
- civil
- passive
- reserved
- group rather than individual centred
- living lives based on consensus rather than confrontation
- trusting
- cautious
- unimaginative.

THE PROS AND CONS OF A JOB IN JAPAN

The pros

- Increasing demand for foreign personnel.
- High rates of remuneration.
- High status of foreign personnel.
- Good fringe benefits for foreign professionals.
- Good career prospects.
- Valuable experience.
- Leading-edge economy.
- Language fluency not essential.
- Law and order.
- Positive discrimination.

The cons

- High population density in major cities.
- Rare cases of negative discrimination.
- High-stress environment.

2
Deciding on your Strategy

CHOOSING A ROUTE TO JAPAN

There are four routes to your job in Japan, each with its own advantages and disadvantages:

1. Finding a job in the UK with Japanese connections.
2. Finding a job in Japan from the UK.
3. Going to Japan and finding your job there.
4. Going to Japan, getting set up first as an English teacher then locating the job you really want.

You must think about which of these routes suits your own personal circumstances. To assist your evaluation, there are four general factors you should consider when deciding which approach is the one for you:

- financial risk
- time taken
- job availability
- competition for jobs.

For each route described, these four factors are considered by a star rating system of one to five, one meaning least and five most.

The best job for you

When it comes to recruiting new talent, the Japanese are no different from any other employer. In the case of senior appointments, they look for experience and a successful track record in the position they wish to fill. Conversely, if the job on offer is a junior post, for what the Japanese call a 'freshman', a Japanese company will not place much emphasis on prior experience, their thinking being that someone coming to the job completely 'fresh' will be easier to train in the business style of their company. In this case, it is qualifications that show your ability and a personality that will fit into their organisation that are the prime considerations. All the same, it is important not to harbour any unrealistic expectations. If your prior experience is working in retailing, then you are no more likely to be considered for a job in finance in Japan than in your own country. Think carefully about your own work experience, qualifications and personality. Bear these in mind when you start your search.

Researching what is available
Your job hunt begins here. Be thorough. Follow up every lead this book provides. Remember, there is a job in Japan for you, but it will not come to you. You will have to find it.

CASE HISTORIES

Karen Stanley
Age:	24.
UK location:	Milton Keynes.
Occupation:	Model.
Qualifications:	Five GCSEs.
Worked:	In Tokyo as a model for eighteen months.

Karen's comments: I would thoroughly recommend Tokyo as a job destination. I got to know the manager of a Japanese modelling agency when he was in London on business and was invited to spend a year on his books. You have to have experience and a decent portfolio to get work in Japan but most important is to have introductions from the right people. The Japanese go for a certain kind of look when they select foreign models for assignments. Generally speaking, they go for blonds, both male and female. Blue eyes are a big plus. If you have the features they like, you can do well even if you haven't done so much work in your local market.

Stuart North
Age:	33.
UK location:	London.
Occupation:	Translator.
Qualifications:	BA Sociology, Royal Society of Arts Preparatory Diploma in Teaching English as a Foreign Language.
Worked:	In Toyko as a teacher before returning to London to join a major electronics company as a translator.

Stuart's comments: I originally went to Japan because I was fed up with life as a state school teacher in the UK. I went out on spec and ended up staying for six years, learning the language while teaching English before changing direction and starting work as a translator. Living in Japan was a great experience and I fully intend to return to live there again in the future. On the other hand, I think it is fair to say that life there isn't for everyone. For people who are very independent and find it hard to work as part of a group, Japan could turn out to be a frustrating experience.

Ken Davies

Age: 23.
UK location: Gloucester.
Occupation: English teacher.
Qualifications: BA English.
Works in: Kita-Kyushu on the Japanese English Teacher (JET) programme.

Ken's comments: I was recruited in England through the JET programme to work as an English teacher for a year in the Japanese state school system. The programme isn't perfect, but on balance, I think there are more pluses than minuses and it is certainly an excellent way to get to know about Japan. When my contract finishes, I shall do what most of the other JET teachers do, that is, stay in Japan and start looking for a job with a Japanese company.

Tony Warren

Age: 31.
UK location: Birmingham.
Occupation: Computer software designer.
Qualifications: BSc Computer Science.
Works in: Saitama Prefecture as a software engineer for a subsidiary of Japan's largest computer manufacturer.

Tony's comments: I was recruited in England through an agent specialising in recruiting for Japanese companies. There is a shortage of experienced software engineers in Japan. I have worked here for almost two years now and picked up quite a lot of the language. The going was tough at first, being in a new country as well as a new job. Companies are set up differently here so there was a lot I had to re-learn. But most of the people around me have been very supportive. I am very happy here and intend to stay for at least another year.

FINDING YOUR JOB IN JAPAN

Broadly speaking, there are four routes that you can take to your job in Japan. Each route possesses its own advantages and disadvantages. The route that you choose (though of course, you can take more than one route) will depend on your priorities, your circumstances and, as some routes present more in the way of challenge and risk than others, your personality.

Before looking in detail at the routes available, ask yourself the following questions and keep the answers in mind while you read through this and the following chapters.

- Do I really want a job in Japan or am I simply looking for a job in the UK with a Japanese company?

- How long am I willing to wait before I get my job in Japan?

- How much money am I willing to invest in finding my job in Japan?

- Do I have sufficient funds available to me?

- Am I prepared to travel to Japan with no job arranged and no guarantee of finding work when I get there?

- Am I willing to contemplate taking temporary work in Japan while hunting down the job that I really want?

- Am I prepared to take a job with a company in the UK with no certainty of being relocated to a position in Japan?

- Am I happy to forego the greater availability and range of jobs in Japan by restricting my search to the UK?

In UK	**Route 2**	**Route 3**	**Route 4**
Route 1 Find a job in the UK with Japanese connections.	Source a job in Japan from the UK.		
Signal your willingness to be relocated to Japan if the chance arises.			
Accept a position in Japan when one becomes available.			
In Japan **Travel to Japan**	**Travel to Japan**	**Travel to Japan** Source a job in country.	**Travel to Japan** Find a temporary job
			Source your permanent position.

Fig.2. Four routes to your job in Japan.

3
Sourcing your Job from the UK

ROUTE 1: FINDING A JOB IN THE UK WITH A JAPANESE CONNECTION

The four factors

Financial risk	*
Time taken	****
Job availability	**
Competition	****

Types of jobs

Jobs with companies in the UK that have a Japanese connection fall into the following three groups:

1. Japanese companies with a branch, subsidiary or joint venture operating in the UK

A wide range of Japanese companies have established a presence in the UK. The range of sectors in which these concerns are active are as follows:

Banking	Securities
Trading	Heavy Engineering
Automotive	Insurance
Chemicals & Pharmaceuticals	Electronics
Finance & Leasing	Construction

2. *UK companies with a branch, subsidiary or joint venture operating in Japan*

The biggest corporate UK presence in Japan occur in the following trade sectors:

Chemicals & Pharmaceuticals	Finance
UK Development Agencies	Law
Engineering	Media
Insurance	Trading
Consumer products	Technology
Education	

3. *Multinationals with operations in the UK and Japan*

With the increasing globalisation of the world's economies, a large number of multinationals have operations both in the UK and Japan. The primary fields in which these companies are active include:

Automotive	Chemicals/Pharmaceuticals
Banking/Finance	Securities
Foods	Media
Information technology	Computers

Comprehensive guides to Japanese companies and institutions operating in the UK, EU companies operating in Japan and multinationals with operations in the UK and Japan appear in the Appendix of this book.

Pros and Cons

The pros

- low financial risk
- broad selection of work available
- gain experience of Japan-related work while in home country
- good benefits when you are sent to a job in Japan as an expatriate
- support with visa applications, relocation expenses etc.

Taking this route means a minimum of financial outlay and there is a wide range of sectors from which to choose. If you have never worked in a company or post with some relation to Japan, you should be able to gain some experience and, perhaps more importantly, some connections which could be to your advantage in the future. If you do get yourself relocated by your company to Japan, you can almost certainly look forward to a healthy package of benefits including paid airfares (probably with paid trips back to the UK for holidays), subsidised accommodation, health insurance and so on. Also, being able to apply for and receive a working visa prior to going to Japan will save a lot of time and bother once you have arrived.

The cons

- greater competition for positions than in Japan
- no guarantee of job in Japan
- relative scarcity of positions in Japan associated with the company.

Conducting your search from the UK means that you will face stiffer competition for the jobs you apply for simply because of the laws of supply and demand. In Japan, as a foreigner, or *gaigin,* you are still a relatively rare commodity, whereas in the UK you could be just another applicant.

Clearly, no employer in the UK will give you a guarantee on entering the company that a vacancy abroad will become available and that if it does, you will be given serious consideration. You could wait a long time for a position even to become available (you are restricting yourself to vacancies arising in only one company) and even then, you have no guarantees that you will be selected for the post.

CASE HISTORY

Name:	Kevin Mitchell.
Age:	34.
Present location:	New York.
Occupation:	Banker specialising in corporate finance.
Qualifications:	BA Economics, MBA.
Worked in:	Tokyo for the branch of a large UK bank that sent him to the post from his previous position with the bank in London.

Kevin's comments: My bank has a policy of rotating some of its specialist staff to branches all over the world. I spent two years in Tokyo and enjoyed every moment. Being a *gaigin* in Japan, whatever you are doing, does tend to make you someone special, certainly more so than London or New York, where you are just another banker in a grey suit. I would have been happy to stay there for longer but I was re-assigned to New

York. Nobody should be under the illusion that a job with a bank is an immediate passport to Japan or anywhere else for that matter. Only around 5 per cent of our staff ever get the chance to take a posting abroad and the competition for those places is murderous.

ROUTE 2: FINDING A JOB IN JAPAN FROM THE UK

The four factors

Financial risk	*
Time taken	****
Job availability	*
Competition	*****

Types of jobs

Generally speaking, job opportunities in Japan that are advertised in the UK are of a specialist nature that require experience and expertise not locally available. There are also a growing number of Japanese multinationals that recruit young talent from the UK with the idea of basing them in Japan for a number of years before relocating them back to the UK to a position of authority in the corporation's UK operation.

Another job sector where jobs are advertised in the UK is in the English teaching trade. Advertisements quite frequently appear, especially around January and February in trade and education publications.

A check of the national broadsheet press and specialist trade journals over one month found jobs in Japan, either with Japanese entities or with foreign companies operating in Japan, being offered in the following sectors:

Electronic consumer goods marketing

Hotel management

Fast moving consumer goods marketing (FMCG)

English teaching

Computer research

Equities trading/analysis

Pros and cons

The pros

- low financial risk

- gain experience of Japan-related work
- better benefits (paid airfares, subsidised accommodation) than for a job found in country
- support with visa applications

As the employer has come looking for you in this case, you will obviously be able to look forward to relatively better pay and conditions. Also, as your employer will almost certainly be Japanese, you should not encounter any bureaucratic problems when applying for your working visa.

The cons

- level of qualifications, experience necessary
- far greater competition for positions than those advertised in Japan
- job opportunities are few and far between
- possible ulterior motives of your employer.

There are as yet only a small number of jobs in Japan advertised in the UK and these tend to be positions with major Japanese corporations, or positions with English schools. The advertisements placed by leading Japanese corporations invariably draw a huge response in terms of applications. One such position advertised through a headhunting agency in one of the major Sunday broadsheets produced nearly 2,500 applications!

The reason for the employer advertising outside Japan is that he can access a far greater supply of *gaigin* talent than is available locally. This means that the company can 'cherry pick' the very best personnel available. As far as you are concerned, that means you will be up against the toughest competition when you make your application.

A word of caution should also be sounded. In some cases, particularly advertisements for positions teaching English in Japan, the employer's reason for canvassing for employees in the UK is purely financial. What sounds like an attractive package of remuneration in the UK, although it may still be quite adequate in Japan, may still be under the 'going rate'. When you arrive in the country, you may find that your contemporaries who have taken jobs after arriving in Japan are being better paid for doing much the same job. The moral is clear: do your homework before committing yourself.

CASE HISTORY

Name: Stella Mason.
Age: 26.

Present location: Toyko.
Occupation: English teacher.
Qualifications: BA Sociology, Royal Society of Arts Preparatory
                  Certificate in Teaching English as a Foreign Language.
Worked in: Ichikawa, Chiba Prefecture as an English teacher after
                  answering an advertisement in the Guardian Education
                  Supplement and attending an interview with the
                  Japanese directors of the school in a London hotel.

Stella's comments: When I got the letter from the school offering me one
of the four teaching positions, I couldn't believe my luck. I really thought
the contract at the school where I was going to teach had to be one of the
best available. I made the mistake of not finding a few people who had
taught in Japan and asking what they thought. When I arrived in Japan
and made a few friends, I soon realised that the conditions I had agreed to
were not as good as I had thought. My monthly salary of 200,000 yen was
comparable to what some others were earning, but I had to work almost
50 per cent more hours to earn it. Other people whom I met who were
teaching English were using their greater free time to do private teaching
and to learn Japanese. The contract I signed included a flat. I had to pay
the rent, but the deposit money was paid by the school. The problem was
that the flat was infested with cockroaches. When I told the school I
wanted to move out, they told me I would have to pay them 250,000 yen
(£1,500) to recompense them for the deposit which they said they would
have to forfeit and three months rent. The contract was for one year
which I worked out, then found another, better-paying job in Tokyo. I did
get a free ticket to Japan (I had to fly on Aeroflot!) but even so, with the
benefit of hindsight, I wish I had done what other people do: come to
Japan on a tourist visa and fix myself up with a job once I had arrived.

SOURCING YOUR JOB IN JAPAN FROM THE UK

Job sourcing from the UK falls broadly into three categories:

- employment agencies
- the UK media
- networking.

Employment agencies

UK agencies such as Manpower and also the more specialised
professional recruitment companies are a good source of positions in UK
companies and multinationals. They also occasionally carry positions in
Japanese companies on their books. The majority of advertised vacancies

within Japanese concerns are, however, advertised by employment agencies specialising in the recruitment of staff for Japanese companies.

Looking at the positions advertised in just one week by one of the larger specialist Japanese recruiters, the following kinds of vacancies were available:

Bond salesmen	Company president	Marketing executive
Maths teacher	Consultant	Personal assistant
Receptionist	Corporate executive	Computer engineer
Sales manager	Equities sales trainee	Research assistant
Warrant salesman	Personnel manager	Forex assistant
Accountant	Systems analyst	Sales assistant
Reservations clerk	Secretarial	PC programmer
Promotions officer	Salesman	

All the major specialist Japanese recruitment agencies plus several UK agencies that offer positions with a Japanese connection are included in the Appendix.

Making an approach to an agency
Recruitment agencies make their money by having the right human material on their books to suit their clients' needs. That means that they very rarely turn down a request by persons wishing to have their details placed on their files. However, just getting your name on the books of an agency does not guarantee that you will receive any offers in the near future. In order to get the most out of any agencies, it is best to follow a few simple steps when making your approach.

1. Telephone the agency and ask to speak to one of the consultants.

2. Explain the kind of work you are looking for and give a brief run down of your qualifications and experience. Ask whether the agency presently has any positions suitable to you. Also, ask to be put on the agency mailing list for vacant positions. (These lists are normally sent out monthly.)

3. Send your CV to the agency addressed to the consultant to whom you spoke.

4. Phone back two or three days later to confirm that your letter arrived and ask again whether there are any new positions that might suit you.

5. Keep phoning the agency regularly (say, once every fortnight or so). Remember that yours is only one amongst a hundred or more files your consultant will be handling. Keeping in contact ensures that the consultant will always have you and your details in mind.

Recruitment agencies are a valuable source of vacant positions but like any other source, you have to work to get the most out of them. Wait for them to call you and the chances are you will be disappointed. If you want your search to be successful, it pays to be methodical.

The media

Vacancies for positions with a Japanese connection do appear in the press, although compared to vacancies in EU nations, they are fairly infrequent. Clearly, the kinds of jobs you will find will be almost exclusively professional positions such as banking and finance, teaching, computing, engineering, etc. It is nevertheless worth looking through the appointments pages of the following broadsheets:

The Times (Wednesday edition in particular).

The Sunday Times Appointments section.

The Times Education Supplement.

The Daily Telegraph (Thursday edition).

The Guardian (Wednesday edition).

The Financial Times (Tuesday edition).

Using professional/trade journals

Japan-related vacancies do appear in professional and trade publications from time to time, particularly in those journals published worldwide. *The Economist,* for example, occasionally carries positions either with Japanese companies or with companies advertising for staff to be located in Japan. The downside, of course, is that *The Economist* boasts a worldwide readership and the competition for those positions advertised will be correspondingly high. Furthermore, positions appearing in these journals will most likely demand very high degrees of qualification and experience.

Career bulletins

A growing number of jobs bulletins are available advertising positions overseas. The majority of these positions seem to be in the Middle East but vacancies do appear for Japan, though mostly in the area of English teaching. Some of the executive jobs bulletins are expensive to subscribe to, but you should be able to persuade the publisher to send you a couple of back numbers so that you can see whether money spent on a subscription would be money well spent. Other bulletins are offered free of charge. You can normally find advertisements for these bulletins in the small ads section of the 'Appointments' pages of the broadsheets and some of the tabloids, such as the *Daily Mail*.

Networking

The Japanese place great value on human relationships, and as such are networkers *par excellence*. For every job found through a recruitment agency or newspaper, there will be many more found through personal recommendation. Moreover, even for jobs advertised through an agency or the press, a personal connection, even a tenuous one, can still prove crucial.

The essential point about networking is getting your name, your abilities and your ambitions known amongst the people who might, at some point in the future, be able to provide you with a recommendation. If your aim is a job in Japan, there are two ways you can start networking.

Networking with Japanese companies in the UK in your chosen field

1. Use the list in the back of this book to get the contact numbers and addresses of companies in your chosen field.

2. Telephone the company and get the name of the personnel director. Get to speak to him/her if you can and introduce yourself.

3. Even if you are told that the company has no positions available at present, send in your CV together with a letter reminding the personnel director about yourself and thanking him/her for taking the time to speak to you over the phone. (Even if you do not speak to anyone in the personnel department, send in your CV anyway, addressed to the personnel director or manager.)

4. Phone again after two or three days. Do not be surprised or disappointed if you receive another negative reply about the lack of appropriate vacancies.

5. Send a second letter a week or so later, thanking the personnel director again for his/her time.

By the time you have completed Step 5, you will have established a network of contacts throughout the Japanese companies in your field. Your name, qualifications and the fact that you are actively seeking a job with them will be in their files. Most importantly, you will have established the fact that you have an interest in their company. You may be lucky and find that a job arises and that your groundwork means that you are considered for the position.

Alternatively, imagine for a moment that you decide that you wish to increase your chances of finding your job in Japan by going there and seeking employment in country. You already have a contact in the UK who can provide you with information (names, numbers, etc.) about the UK company's parent in Japan. Before you go to Japan, contact the personnel officer once more and get him/her to provide you with a contact name in the personnel department of the company's head office (or branch, if it is a foreign company) in Japan. Now you have the makings of a second network. Most importantly, when you go to Japan and contact the company concerned, you will be able to give the name of the personnel director in the UK company as a reference to show that rather than just canvassing the parent company on the off chance, your enquiry is part of a relationship you have already established in the UK.

It is worth repeating again that for the Japanese, personal recommendation and connections are very important. If you do things the Japanese way and start to network, you can only improve your chances of success.

Note: *Using a Japanese CV*
Japanese employers expect their potential employees to be able to integrate well into a Japanese company and environment. Clearly, showing from the beginning that you are prepared to do things the Japanese way can only be an advantage. One way in which you can display this willingness is by sending in a Japanese-style curriculum vitae. A sample Japanese CV is shown in Fig. 3. Japanese CVs do not vary considerably, all following the same basic format. In Japan, they are available from any stationers. In the UK, they can be purchased at

shops specialising in Japanese products such as the Japan Centre at 212 Piccadilly, London W1. While you may not be able to write Japanese yourself, you will certainly be able to find someone Japanese willing to assist you.

Networking through associations and foundations
A considerable number of these bodies exist in the UK designed to foster greater communication and understanding between Japan and the UK. A list is provided in the Appendix. Some of these associations deal with specific fields, such as the Electronic Industries Association of Japan, while others provide a more general nexus for meeting and the exchange of information and opinions, such as the Nippon Club. All these bodies provide the chance to meet with Japanese to start your own informal network of connections and introductions.

SPECIAL ROUTES TO YOUR JOB IN JAPAN

The European Commission Executive Training Programme
Since 1979, the Japan Division of the European Commission has operated an eighteen-month training programme aimed at equipping company executives from EU member states with the linguistic ability and cultural know how to do business in Japan. The stated aim of the course is to help bring down the huge deficit in trade between the EU and Japan. The Executive Training Programme (ETP) consists of a 12-month intensive language course during which time weekly seminars on Japanese business practice and culture are held. There are also company visits and at least one homestay during this period. The first year is followed by a 6-month in-house training period with one or two Japanese companies in a field related to that in which the executive works in his or her own company. Over 500 business people have undertaken the ETP course since its inception.

Qualifying for participation in ETP
- The applicant must work for an EU member state company already exporting to Japan or with a convincing marketing strategy for developing a market in Japan.
- The applicant must be qualified to degree level.
- Age range is 25-37 although extension is possible in special cases.
- At least two years work experience is necessary, preferably including a period overseas.

履　歴　書　　　　1994年　7月　20日現在

No.＿＿＿＿＿＿

| ふりがな | | | | | ※男・女 | |
| 氏　名 | マイケル・ターナー | | | | 印 | |

1961年　4月　5日生
（満　33　歳）　本籍　英国　※都道府県

ふりがな		電話 市外局番（03　）
現住所 （〒　）	東京都 中野区 東中野 1-1-1	3771 1234 （　　方呼出）
ふりがな		電話 市外局番（　　）
連絡先（現住所以外に連絡を希望する場合のみ記入） （〒　　－　　）		（　　方呼出）

年	月	学歴・職歴など（項目別にまとめて書く）
		学　　歴
1972-79		メイドストーン スクール フォー ボーイズ
1979-82		ケンブリッジ ユニバーシティ
1982-84		マンチェスター ユニバ・シティ
		職　　歴
1984-88		IBM
1988-93		アップル コンピューター カンパニー
1993～		NEC

記入上の注意　①鉛筆以外の青または黒の筆記具で記入。　②数字はアラビア数字で、文字はくずさず正確に書く。
③※印のところは、該当するものを○で囲む。

Fig. 3. (1 of 2) Sample Japanese CV.

No._____

身上書

年　　月　　日現在

ふりがな

氏　名：　マイケル・ベーカー

現住所（〒　　　－　　　）：東京都中野区東中野 ーノーー

電話
市外局番（ 63 ）
3772 - 1234
（　　　方呼出）

年	月	免　許　・　資　格
1979		Ａレベル，数学・物理・コンピューター技術
1982		BSc ・ 数学
1984		Msc ・ コンピューター
1992		MBA ・ ビジネス

得意な学科
　数学

趣　味
　音楽・興曲鑑賞

スポーツ
　テニス・ラグビー

健康状態
　良好

志望の動機
　貴社の業務が自己の
　性格に最適

	氏　　名	性　別	生年月日	氏　　名	性　別	生年月日
家			・　・			・　・
			・　・			・　・
族			・　・			・　・
			・　・			・　・
			・　・			・　・

本人希望記入欄（特に給料・職種・勤務時間・勤務地その他について希望があれば記入）

　東京電機，コンピューター開発関係希望。

保護者（本人が未成年者の場合のみ記入）
ふりがな

氏　名：

住所（〒　　　－　　　）

電話
市外局番（　　　）
（　　　方呼出）

採用者側の記入欄（志望者は記入しないこと）

日本法令　労務12-2　55.11.改

Fig. 3. (2 of 2) Sample Japanese CV.

What you receive

A grant of ECU 110,000 is available for all first-time participants in the scheme. This sum covers all course costs and also provides a settling-in allowance of 600,000 yen (approximately £3,900) plus a monthly living allowance of 400,000 yen (approximately £2,600) for the entire eighteen-month period. The grant is the same for all applicants regardless of age and marital status. It is usual for the successful applicant's employer to top up the grant in order to make the applicant's stay in Japan more comfortable as well as providing support for any remaining commitments in the UK, such as mortgage repayments. Travel costs are not covered by the ETP grant.

Making an application

Applications are made through PA Consulting Group by the employee wishing to be considered for the scheme. An interview with the candidate and his or her employer takes place with successful applicant's details then being forwarded to the European Commission. Applications made in June are sent to the Commission in August and candidates are screened by the Commission in December. Successful candidates start the ETP course in May of the following year.

The addresses of PA Consulting's EU branch offices can be found in the Appendix.

Doing scientific research

There are three main ways of spending time in Japan doing scientific research. Be aware, however, that these opportunities are usually limited to holders of doctoral degrees.

1. *The Japan Society for the Promotion of Science*
   The Society offers fifty post-doctoral fellowships annually.

2. *The Japanese Science and Technology Agency*
   The Agency offers financial support to young researchers wishing to conduct research at a Japanese national laboratory with the exception of those laboratories that are affiliated to a national university.

3. *The National Science Foundation*
   The Tokyo office of the Foundation provides a directory of more than 120 Japanese companies willing to support foreign scientists wishing to do research in Japan.

The Japanese Education & Exchange (JET) programme

Since 1987, the JET programme has offered young graduates the chance of a year's contract working as an Assistant English Teacher (AET) or a Co-ordinator for International Relations (CIT) in Japan. As the title suggests, AETs work in Japanese schools as assistants to Japanese teachers of English. CITs, on the other hand, work with the local community, liaising and co-ordinating with foreign organisations and generally helping with the smooth flow of international relations.

Most of these posts are offered not in the metropolises but in the provincial cities of Japan. For those wishing to experience the 'real' Japan, this may be an advantage. For people who seek life in the big city and see the JET programme as a stepping stone to work in a Japanese corporation in Tokyo or Osaka, being assigned to an outlying region where there is very little industry may be a frustrating experience. Nevertheless, with over 3,000 positions available annually (and a regular shortfall in applications of 20 per cent), the JET programme is certainly something you should look into.

Conditions of application

Nationality:	The JET programme is open to applications from citizens of the following countries: UK, Eire, USA, Canada, Australia and New Zealand.
Language:	you must be a native speaker of English.
Age:	under 35.
Qualifications:	university degree.
Other:	some interest in Japan.
Period:	one year from 1 August to 31 July.

The pros

- demand for people to fill these positions outstrips applications
- sponsored by the Japanese Ministry of Education
- moderately good salary
- contract renewable by mutual consent
- accommodation found
- assistance with visa application.

The cons

- limited nature of work
- assigned area may be unsuitable to your personality.

CASE HISTORIES

Name:	Martin Jaworski.
Age:	27.
UK location:	Derbyshire.
Occupation:	Martin now works for a major Japanese automobile manufacturer.
Qualifications:	BA Economics.
Worked in:	Nagoya, Central Japan

Martin's comments: I went to Japan on the JET scheme as an AET in 1989. My only prior knowledge of the country was a unit I had studied on the Japanese economy as part of my degree. I was assigned to work at several schools north of Nagoya in an area where there were almost no other *gaigin*. As such, I was something of a celebrity, though after the first month, the novelty of the constant attention began to wear off and I began to feel rather isolated. The work itself did not really agree with me. As I worked through the week at several schools, I really never had much of a chance to get to know any of the staff and certainly no chance to get to know any of the children, who in any case, could hardly communicate in English. The first couple of months were without doubt one of the most lonely times of my life. I can't fault the Japanese, who were wonderfully hospitable but even so, I really did consider chucking it all in more than once. After the first months had gone by and I had made the acquaintance of some foreigners in Nagoya, along with some Japanese who I found I could feel more comfortable with, things started to look up. The rest of the year flew by. At the end of the contract, I was offered an extension but politely declined as I had already fixed myself up with one of Japan's biggest car makers, who were on the point of opening a large plant in the UK. I worked for them in Nagoya for eighteen months before being posted back to England to work at their new plant. I don't think the JET scheme is for everyone, certainly not for those who are uneasy being so conspicuous.

Name:	Jackie Barrington.
Age:	24.
UK location:	London.
Occupation:	Works for a travel company.
Qualifications:	BA Sociology.
Worked in:	Shikoku.

Jackie's comments: I went out on the JET scheme in July 1992. It only took me a week to realise I had made a mistake. I had never taught before, so I was unprepared to be put in front of class after class of forty and more, unresponsive middle and high school students. I felt that I had to be the first foreigner some of the people on the island of Shikoku had ever seen. I suppose I failed to cope but after six weeks, I decided enough was enough and told the local co-ordinator of the JET programme that I wanted to return to the UK. Since returning to England and talking with other people who have lived in Japan, I think I made a mistake coming back so soon. Everyone, it seems, finds the first few months quite tough because everything is so different. It's very easy to talk with the benefit of hindsight, but I wish now I had stuck it out for a couple of months at least and made my decision then.

VISA APPLICATIONS

The visa process for persons travelling to Japan to take up employment is quite straightforward and this fact alone makes securing a job before going to Japan very advantageous.

The first steps

It falls to your new employer to make an application at the Ministry of Justice, or *houmu-sho*, for a Certificate of Eligibility, or *zairyu shikaku nintei shomei-sho*. Without this certificate you will not be granted a working visa. Once your employer has completed this process, he or she must send the original of the certificate to you.

Over to you

All applications for Japanese working visas are made at the Consulate General of Japan. It is not necessary for the application to be made in your own country. As long as you produce the necessary documentation, your work visa can be processed at any Japanese Consulate.

What you need to take

The required documentation is as follows:
- a valid passport
- one visa application form completed and signed by yourself
- one passport-sized photograph
- the original of the Certificate of Eligibility plus one photocopy.

The Consulate General of Japan in London states that in certain cases, 'additional documents in support of your application will be required.' This condition is usually applied when there is some doubt over the authenticity of your Certificate of Eligibility or your employer.

Timing your application

The time taken to process your application can vary from one week to up to two months in some, albeit rare, cases. Nevertheless, as it is always better to err on the side of caution, apply for your work visas two months prior to leaving for Japan if this is possible.

What you get

You will receive a visa, normally for a period of one year, although some people have only received visas for six months. No matter if your contract in Japan is for two or three years, your visa will extend only to one year and so must be renewed (prior to expiry) if you stay in Japan longer than the first twelve-month term.

Renewing your visa

If you are unlucky enough to receive only a six-month visa, or if you decide to extend your stay in Japan, you will need to apply for a visa renewal. This is best done at least two weeks prior to the expiry date of your original visa.

Where to go

Visa renewal applications are dealt with at the Immigration Bureau of the Ministry of Justice. A list detailing all the principal branches of the bureau around Japan is included in the Appendix of this book.

What you need to make your application

Renewing your visa requires the submission of the following documents, which are in fact the same documents as your employer submitted for your Certificate of Eligibility prior to you applying for your original working visa:

- The company registration form or *tohon,* of the company that is employing you.

- Your contract of employment or *keiyaku-sho.*

- A certificate of employment or *kyuyo-hosho-sho,* stating the terms and conditions of your contract.

- The company tax certificate or *nozei shomei-sho.*

- A letter of guarantee or *hosho-sho,* from the company employing you. (The company must commit itself to pay for your return trip home if it is decided that you are an undesirable.)

- Company brochure or annual report, *annai-sho.*

- A list of employees currently with the company.
- Two black and white passport photographs.
- Your CV.
- Your degree certificates and other qualifications.

How long does it take?

Your visa is renewed while you wait, as long as no problems occur, such as a lack of the proper documentation. The branches of the *homu-sho* are usually very undermanned which means that while the process itself is fairly straightforward, you may have to wait three, four, even five hours for your visa to be renewed. It is a good idea to plan ahead and get to the *homu-sho* as early as you can, thereby being one of the first applications to be processed before the over-worked staff are snowed under by applications.

What you get

You may be tempted to apply for a longer visa than the period granted you when you originally applied, particularly if you were only awarded a six-month visa. There is no regulation preventing you from doing this but it is almost certain that the *homu-sho* official will ignore your request for a longer visa and renew your visa for the same period as that of the original. If you question this, you will receive one of a stock of reasons that all the officials seem to have learned by heart. One thing is clear, no matter how much you try to persuade the official to have a change of heart and grant your request, his/her decision is final. This decision may well be that your six-month visa means you will have to waste another day in six months time making yet another application for renewal, but there is sadly nothing you can do about it except take the chance to learn an important part of Japanese thinking and *gaman suru,* meaning to 'grin and bear it.'

Some Do's and Don'ts with Japanese bureaucracy

Despite accusations of partiality and the sometimes seeming arbitrary nature of decisions, the processing and issuing of Japanese work visas is done fairly, and most of the time efficiently. The Japanese do things by the book. That means that if you have forgotten a form, or if the official registering your application is unhappy with some of the documentation you have provided, it will be up to you and your employer to satisfy his requirements.

- Do be polite. The bureau is undermanned and the officials are usually snowed under with applications. Don't make their life any harder than it already is.

- Do accept the official's decision.
- Do as you are requested.
- Don't try to insist that your application is processed anyway.
- Do resist the temptation to get angry or flustered if a problem occurs.
- Don't try to persuade the official to make an exception.

APPLYING FOR YOUR REGISTRATION CARD

The work visa in your passport will be stamped on your arrival in Japan. The process is not over yet, however. It is now your responsibility to register your residence at your city office, *shiyaku-sho*, or ward office, or *kuyaku-sho*, if you live in one of the large wards of a major city like Tokyo or Osaka. When you have registered, you will receive your foreigner registration card or *gaigin touroku-sho*. Do as regulations require and keep your *gaigin* card with you at all times. If you do not, and you are stopped by the police, you will be detained at the local police station until someone can go to your home or office and bring the police your card, an embarrassment and a potential waste of time that is easily avoided. A sample application form of a *gaigin touroku-sho* is shown in Fig. 4.

When to apply
You must register within ninety days of your arrival in Japan. It is best to register as quickly as you can.

What you will need

- your passport
- four passport photographs
- a fingerprint for identification purposes.

The process

1. You hand your documents in at the reception counter where an official checks you have provided everything necessary for your application to be processed.

2. You will be given a numbered ticket and told to take your documents (now held in a plastic folder) to one of the officials dealing with the applications.

3. When you submit your documents, the official will put your folder

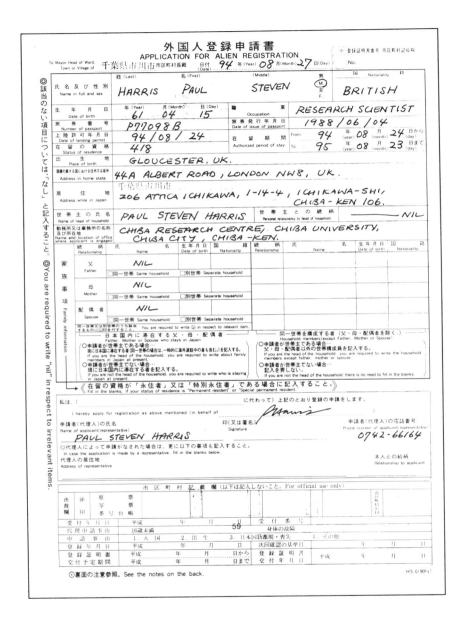

Fig. 4. Sample foreigner registration card application form.

at the bottom of the pile of applications he is currently processing.

4. Now all you have to do is wait. When the official comes to your documents he will process them and call your number. You go to his/her counter with your passport, which is then stamped with a fresh work visa. The official may ask you some questions (first in Japanese, then in English if you can't reply in Japanese) just to confirm who you are and what you are doing in Japan. Alternatively, he/she may just stamp your passport and hand it back to you. The *homu-sho* gets to keep all the documents submitted with your application. The whole process takes on average around two to two and a half hours, depending on how many other foreigners are trying to get their visas renewed at the same time as you.

You will be required to fill out a form stating your identity and providing information about your home address and your employer. The *gaigin* card is issued to you there and then. A sample card is shown in Fig. 5. Remember that this card is only valid for the same period as your visa. Therefore, when you renew your visa six months or a year down the road, you will also have to pay another visit to your local *shi-* or *kuyaku-sho* to renew your *gaigin* card. This is, as the Japanese say, very *mendo-kusai* or troublesome. But there is really nothing you can do about this, except to *gaman suru*.

RE-ENTRY PERMITS

It is dangerous to assume that once you have been granted your work permit, you are free to travel to and from Japan at will. This would be a grave mistake. Once you have gone through immigration procedures on arrival and your work permit has been stamped, you cannot then leave the country without invalidating your work permit. In order to be able to travel to and from Japan without doing this, you must apply for another permit, the re-entry permit.

What the re-entry permit does

The re-entry permit allows you to leave Japan and return without having to re-apply for a new work visa. There are two types of permit, single and multiple, which as their titles suggest permit one return trip from Japan and multiple return trips from Japan respectively. A single re-entry permit costs 2,000 yen and a multiple 4,000. Needless to say, most people opt for the multiple re-entry permit. While your application is being processed, you use the money to buy either a 2,000 or 4,000 yen revenue stamp which

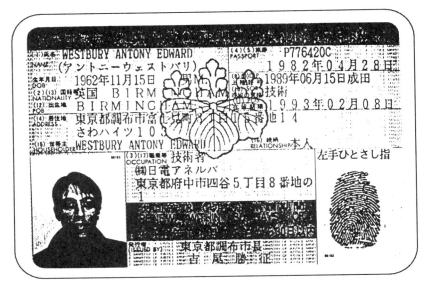

Fig. 5. Sample foreigner registration card.

you stick to a form which the official selling the stamp will give you. You simply print and sign your name on the form and hand it in when your application has been processed. The permits are valid for the same period as your working visa, which means that when your visa comes up for renewal, you must also renew your re-entry permit if you wish to make trips out of the country.

Where you get it
Re-entry permits are obtained from the place where you apply for work permit renewals, the Immigration Bureau of the Ministry of Justice, or *homu-sho*.

What you will need to apply

- your passport
- an application form which you take from the processing counter
- the 2,000 or 4,000 yen revenue stamp affixed to a completed and signed application form.

Things to remember

1. Like the procedure for visa renewal, applications are dealt with on a ticketing system. Therefore, try to get your ticket from the machine as

soon as you can to guarantee that your processing will be done as quickly as possible.

2. The re-entry permit, used or unused, single or multiple, is only valid for the length of your current visa. This means that when your work permit comes up for renewal, you would also be wise to renew your re-entry visa at the same time.

3. To save yourself time, when you go to the *homu-sho* to renew your working visa, submit the documents for your visa renewal, then make your way to the office dealing with re-entry visas (it should be just down the corridor) and get your application for the re-entry permit underway while your visa renewal application is being processed. Doing it this way should save you an hour or two.

ROUTE 3: FINDING YOUR JOB AFTER ARRIVAL IN JAPAN
The four factors

Financial risk	****
Time taken	**
Job availability	****
Competition	**

Going to Japan to find your job represents a financial risk, there are no two ways about it. At the very least, you should not consider going to Japan with the idea of finding work with funds of less than £2,000. This may seem like a lot of money to gamble, but remember that the odds are weighted in your favour and the increased access to the Japanese jobs market makes it a risk well worth taking.

Pros and cons

The pros

- access to far bigger and broader market of jobs
- greater demand for foreign talent than supply
- reduced time necessary to find your job
- better benefits than jobs advertised abroad in some cases
- sense of achievement.

The cons

- finance necessary to fund trip and first weeks in Japan
- greater element of risk
- more complicated visa procedure
- stress related to job hunting in a strange environment.

CASE HISTORY

Name:	Celia Grech.
Age:	27.
UK location:	London.
Occupation:	Journalist.
Qualifications:	BA History.
Works in:	Tokyo, where she has lived since arriving in Japan two years ago.

Celia's comments: I wanted to get work experience somewhere in Asia and after doing some research, decided that Japan was the best place for me to head in terms of demand for news material and the availability of other work (i.e. English teaching) if the worst came to the worst and I couldn't get set up quickly in something media-related. As it happened, I need not have worried as I was lucky enough to pick up an assistant editorial job with an American news magazine in just under a month. I think the reason I got the job was that I did my homework beforehand, found out where and with whom I had to start networking when I arrived in Tokyo. I have since changed jobs as my long-term aim is to support myself completely from freelancing but one thing I have realised is that there is quite a lot of work here just as long as you keep a finger on the pulse and know where to find it.

ROUTE 4: FINDING YOUR JOB IN JAPAN WHILE DOING TEMPORARY WORK

The four factors:

Financial risk	***
Time taken	**
Job availability	*****
Competition	**

Route 4 represents a compromise. By taking a temporary job (which will probably be English teaching) you are buying yourself time to find the position you came to Japan to take up and at the same time you are reducing the amount of money you need to bring with you to get yourself set up. There are other temporary job possibilities such as aerobics teaching, sports coaching, etc., but the greatest source of stop-gap work is in the language trade, teaching English to the Japanese.

Pros and cons

The pros

- less finance necessary
- more time to find the job that really suits you
- good supply of interim teaching jobs
- less stress through less risk of failure
- increased possibility of networking your way to a job.

The cons

- doing work that you may not like
- more complicated visa procedure.

CASE HISTORY

Name:	Chris Simpson.
Age:	26.
UK location:	Hemel Hempstead
Occupation:	Works in a small Japanese trading company.
Qualifications:	BA Economics and Law.
Works in:	Osaka, where he has lived for the past year.

Chris's comments: I left university and went to work as a trainee manager in a high street shopping chain. After a year, I made up my mind that it wasn't for me so I left and decided to do some travelling. After four months in Asia, I ended up in Japan rather short on funds and looking for a ticket home. I met a Japanese man in a bar, of all places, who said he was looking for someone to teach English at a school he owned and would I be interested. So I ended up with a visa sponsor and a job teaching English in Japan completely by accident. Unfortunately, I found that teaching English wasn't up my street. After six months I'd had enough of sitting in front of a class of unresponsive housewives and high school children who were always half asleep. Having said that, the job did give me the chance to get myself set up with an apartment in Osaka and enough time to start learning the language. I decided to join two agencies that deal with Japanese companies looking for foreign staff. Three months and four interviews later, I started working for a small Japanese trading company. I feel like a bit of a general dogsbody at times, but as I'm starting from the bottom up that's something I have to accept and as I get treated no differently from the young Japanese men who work there, I don't really have anything to complain about. There's no doubt that working in Japan is a challenge, but I'm determined to stay put until I've got a lot more experience under my belt.

FINDING YOUR JOB IN JAPAN

The three primary sources of jobs once you have arrived in Japan are the same as in the UK:

- employment agencies
- the media
- networking.

Employment agencies

There are a considerable number of employment agencies, particularly in Tokyo, that specialise in the placement of foreign personnel, both in Japanese companies and in foreign companies with branches and subsidiaries in Japan. It is in the interests of the employer to hire staff in Japan because doing this usually means they can offer benefits packages lower than those they would have to offer if they were hiring personnel from abroad. The advantage of this, as far as you are concerned, is that there will be a much larger supply of positions available than you would find in the UK.

A telephone call to one of the biggest of these agencies revealed that they had the following kinds of positions available on their books.

Japanese share salesmen (J)	Customer dealers (J)
Swap assistants	Computer programmer (AS400)
Information system salesmen (J)	Trading company managers (engineering)
Personal assistants	
	Computer system engineers
Equity research assistants (J)	
	Futures analysts (J)
Hotel managers	

Positions followed by (J) are those that required Japanese language ability. The company stressed that as well as permanent positions, they also held a large number of temporary contracts on their books (six months to one year.)

Making an approach to an agency

As in the UK, recruitment agencies prosper by their ability to provide their clients with the right people. The supply of the 'right people' is very much at a premium in Tokyo, so in many cases clients are willing to compromise to fill a position rather than wait for the perfect candidate, who may never appear, or go to the far greater expense of hiring from abroad. That means you have a much better chance of success working through an agency in Tokyo than you would have if you limited yourself to London agencies.

Nevertheless, the same rules still apply. You won't get anywhere unless you persevere, or as the Japanese say, *ganbatte*. In order to show that you not only possess the experience and qualifications but also the willpower and motivation to succeed, keep in contact with the agency even if your first approach does not turn up anything that is suitable. Remember, the positions on offer change daily and a three-minute call to see what new positions have come in will cost you nothing more than the yen equivalent of fifty pence.

1. Telephone the agency and ask to speak to one of the consultants.

2. Explain the kind of work you are looking for and give a brief run down of your qualifications and experience. Ask whether the agency presently has any positions suitable to you. Normally, the agency will ask you to visit them for an exploratory interview. Make sure you get clear directions and ask which station is the closest to their offices.

3. Attend the interview, taking along your CV and any supporting documents such as certificates, letters of reference, etc.

4. If the agency has any positions on file that the consultant thinks are relevant, he will ask whether you wish to be considered for them. If your answer is positive, he will send a copy of your details along to the personnel department of the company in question. If their response is also positive, then a first interview will be arranged between you and the company in question.

5. If there are no suitable vacancies at the time of your interview, remember to keep in contact. You never know when the situation will change.

The media

A wide range of vacancies for foreigners appear in the English language press in Japan. The majority of these jobs are still in the field of English teaching but this situation is changing, and as you can imagine, if the job you are looking for does not materialise quickly, English teaching can become a very valuable stop-gap source of funds while you continue your search. English teaching should not be underestimated - it can be the difference between you getting the job you want and having to fly home when the funds run out.

The English language press in Japan comprises English language versions of Japan's major dailies, namely:

The Daily Yomiuri
The Daily Mainichi
The Asahi Evening News

plus the specialist English language newspaper:

The Japan Times.

All of the above publications run quite extensive classified sections. Without doubt, the best of all is the Monday edition of the *Japan Times* which carries four to five pages full of new positions every week.

Other English language papers available in Japan and worth looking through are:

The Financial Times
The Asian Wall Street Journal
The Far Eastern Economic Review
The Nikkei International.

Following up newspaper advertisements
Work through the newspapers, putting a ring around every advertisement that you think has some potential. Telephone the number included in the advertisement as soon as possible. Some of these jobs tend to go to one of the first people who answer the ad, so be as quick as you can. If the company that placed the advertisement is interested in you, they will ask you along to an interview, probably the same day or the day after.

Networking

In Japan, connections, or *kone,* as the Japanese call them, are a huge advantage in the hunt for work. Many Japanese companies, and not a few foreign companies operating in Japan, use their *kone* as their primary channel when they are looking for new employees. Moreover, in many cases, companies do not have positions waiting to be filled *per se,* but are nevertheless always on the lookout for talent. You should set about establishing your own network of *kone* as soon as possible after arriving in Japan. This is not so difficult as it may seem to you, coming to Japan for the first time. You may already have started networking back in England by contacting Japanese companies and other companies with interests in Japan. The next step in the process is to use those contacts and to start developing others.

Networking through associations and foundations
The quickest networking route to your job in your chosen field is to research what professional and trade associations related to your work exist in Japan and go along and start meeting people. There are a large number of such organisations in Japan and a comprehensive list of their names, addresses and contact numbers is included in the Appendix. Associations exist in the following fields:

English Teaching	Public Relations
Foreign Law	Architecture
Journalism	Broadcasting
Advertising	Computing
Scientific Research	Travel/Tourism
Translation	

Attending the meetings of these associations means that you gain access not only to a wealth of inside information on jobs but also hundreds of years worth of experience of working and social life in Japan. It can be very reassuring to find that you are doing something which many other people have successfully done before you. Not only that, but the opportunity to start meeting people and make friends will mark the beginning of your new life in Japan.

Using the network you started in the UK

1. Research the addresses and telephone numbers of the Japanese head offices and foreign branches of the companies you included in your UK network.

2. Telephone the companies and speak to the person whose name you were given in the UK. Explain who you are and the kind of position you are seeking. Do not forget to explain that you have been in contact with the company's operation in the UK and make a point of

mentioning the name of the personnel director or manager who dealt with you. You may be asked at this point to attend an interview or alternatively, simply to provide further details about yourself, your qualifications and experience.

3. Send in your CV and other relevant documentation.

4. After two days, telephone back to the person you spoke to when you made your first call. Again, you may be asked to attend an interview. Alternatively, you may be told there are no suitable positions available at present. In this case don't be disappointed. You have established another *kone,* and at some point in the not too distant future, your networking will pay a dividend.

MAKING A DECISION

The day will come when you will have to decide whether or not you need to contemplate taking an English teaching job in order to enable you to continue your search for the job you wish to take up. The timing of this decision will depend to a large extent on whether or not you have enough finances available to continue your search without needing to replenish your supply of money. There is a good supply of English teaching jobs in Japan and in many cases, experience is not considered a necessary condition of employment as many schools actually prefer teachers who have no previous teaching background, thinking that this gives the teacher a 'fresher' approach. Rather than wanting a teacher in the accepted sense of the word, most Japanese want a native speaker with whom to practise their English in Japan, so you should be able to pick up a job quite quickly. It is worth remembering that many of the people who come to your classes will be businessmen. Your lessons will become another opportunity for you to develop some *kone* and network your way to the job you are looking for.

Be careful, however, to budget for your life in Tokyo up until the day when you receive your first month's salary. As a rule of thumb, if you have been in Tokyo for two weeks and have not yet found anything you feel suits you, it could be time to turn your attention to tracking down a teaching job you can do to keep you solvent during the interim.

Finding a job teaching English
There are two methods you can use to find a teaching position.

Newspaper advertisements
You will find a lot of advertisements, particularly in the *Japan Times,* from schools requiring English teachers.

Cold calling
It is always worth calling the larger English schools to check whether or not they have a need for extra staff. The turnover rate in some of the bigger schools is fairly high (like you, other people use English teaching as a stepping stone to another occupation) and there is always the chance that you will call at the right moment. Use the list of English language schools provided in the Appendix to conduct your search.

Looking at other options
English teaching is not the only recourse but it is the easiest and most plentiful work you will find and often the best paid. But if you think your talents would be better used in other fields, there are alternative jobs that you may track down in the classified pages of the English language dailies, including the following:

Sports coaching
Normally tennis or golf. Obviously experience is necessary. Language ability is not always essential as many companies advertising for coaches like to combine coaching with English language practice for their clientele. Speaking some Japanese is usually an advantage. The type of people you are likely to meet would certainly be good for your network or *kone.*

Aerobics/gym training
Again, most companies require prior experience. Basic Japanese language ability is normally considered advantageous.

Hostessing
For women, this is another option worth considering. Hostessing forms part of what the Japanese call the 'water trade' or *mizu-shobai.* As such, the work is not considered to be quite respectable and certainly there are frequent cases of women being forced into prostitution. However, these cases almost always involve South East Asian women working in Japan illegally. The advertisements appearing in the English language press are almost always from bona fide establishments in the best parts of Tokyo such as Ginza and Akasaka. Being a hostess means evening work, usually from 6.00 p.m. until midnight or later. Pay is usually competitive with that of English teaching with the added benefit that your days will be free to

pursue other employment opportunities. Advertisements will state whether Japanese ability is necessary.

INTERVIEWS

Whatever job you take in Japan, whether it be a position teaching English or as a manager in a Japanese company, you will have to attend an interview. There are certain basic rules that you need to observe to ensure that your first meeting with your potential employer does not fail even before it has begun.

Making the right impression

- Dress for success.
- Be punctual.
- Do your homework.
- Be patient.
- Be yourself.
- Knowing the Do's and Don'ts.

Dress for success

One thing you will soon realise after arrival in Japan is that the Japanese lay great stress on appearance and on form. Japanese workers, no matter what their job, will be dressed cleanly and tidily. Housewives out doing their shopping will be dressed so that they would not look out of place in the lounge of one of Tokyo's top hotels. Above all, the Japanese are a people who like to confirm to codes of dress and feel uncomfortable being conspicuous. Whether or not you would feel similarly uncomfortable, you should nevertheless make the effort to abide by their rules if you want to be successful in your search for a job.

Following the dress codes
Men attending an interview for a job with a Japanese company should dress conservatively:

Suit:	Dark blue or charcoal grey, preferably single breasted.
Shirt:	Plain white, if possible. Otherwise pale blue.
Tie:	Plain or striped, nothing loudly designed.
Shoes:	Black, plain Oxford or Brogue.

Furthermore, any kind of facial hair is frowned upon in Japanese society. Go to your interview clean shaven. No moustaches, no beards and a conservative hairstyle.

The same kind of conservatism applies to women, who should wear something close to the following:

Suit: Dark blue, or alternatively, blue blazer with skirt. No trousers.

Blouse: White or cream.

Shoes: Black, simply styled with medium or low heels.

Clearly for some occupations, such as English teaching or sports coaching, such formal standards of dress are not obligatory. Nevertheless, you should present yourself looking clean and tidy in clothes that are neither overly bright nor show signs of wear. It should be noted that temperature and humidity vary dramatically in Japan depending on the season. If you find yourself in Tokyo in June or July, you will need very thin, natural fibre based clothing to help you cope with the heat and dampness. Conversely, in winter time, there will be days when you will need an overcoat on top of your vest, shirt and wool jacket to keep the cold out.

Scoring marks for presentation

As already mentioned above, the Japanese lay great stress on appearance. Your CV and other supporting documents should be presented for inspection in a A4-sized manila envelope. If you present the interviewer with a Japanese CV, it should be a handwritten original not a photocopy.

Arriving on time

Japan's cities can be very confusing places to the uninitiated. Street names and numbers do not exist. Instead, the cities are divided into a number of wards, or -ku. Each -ku is subdivided into a number of cho-me, and the cho-me further sub-divided into banchi, which are divided further into smaller banchi. Lastly, most office blocks have names which form the final piece of the puzzle.

A typical Tokyo address would, for example, read as follows:

> ABC Corporation,
> 5F, Muromachi Building,
> 2-4-3 Nihombashi,
> Chuo-ku,
> Tokyo 103.

The numbers 2-4-3 correspond to the cho-me, banchi and sub-divided banchi. The area is Chuo ward in central Tokyo. The final number, 103, is the Japanese version of a postal code. As you might have guessed, the

Japanese system of addresses is somewhat imprecise and it is not only foreigners newly arrived in Japan who have problems finding their way around. Therefore, it is important that you do the following to ensure that you do not make the mistake of arriving late for your interview.

1. Get someone at the company, or *kaisha,* you are visiting to tell you the name of the nearest subway station and also which exit from the station you should take. (Some of the largest subway stations in Tokyo and Osaka have ten or more exits so it is vital you know which one to use.) Also, ask for directions from the exit to the office building where the *kaisha* is located.

2. Use a map of Tokyo to locate the station and also the *-ku* and *-cho-me* in which the address is located. (Most good Japanese city maps will have the *-ku* and *-cho-me* marked out.) If the building in which the *kaisha* you are visiting has its offices is a big one, then this may also be marked on the map.

3. On the day of your interview, leave early enough to cope with lost time in the event that you get lost.

4. If you cannot find the address, the best place to go for help is the nearest police box, or *Koban.* These are located all over the cities and towns of Japan. You will invariably find one outside the main exits of most subway stations. Even if the policeman inside does not speak much English, he will have at his disposable very detailed street maps of the district you are in and should be able to point you in the right direction.

5. If you cannot find a *Koban,* ask someone in the street. The best people to ask will be younger businessmen who should be able to speak some English. As you are in Japan, anyone you ask will do their very best to help their *gaigin* guest.

Being yourself

The Japanese interview system is designed to enable your employers to get as good a picture of you as possible before taking any decisions. At the same time, you have the opportunity to develop a picture of what life will be like inside the company without committing yourself. If you find yourself becoming irritated or annoyed by the manner of the people you are dealing with, it would be wise to take that as a signal that life in a Japanese company might not be for you. Working at a *kaisha* is clearly not for everyone and there are many stories of people who joined Japanese organisations only to leave a few weeks or months later, angry and disillusioned with their experience. The interview process for a Japanese company has been compared to a betrothal. If you begin to get the feeling that you have chosen the wrong partner, think very carefully before going any further.

Being prepared

Some foreigners have likened Japanese interview techniques to an inquisition. It is without doubt a very thorough process, designed not only to learn as much as possible about your character and suitability before you join the company, but also to determine your potential level of commitment. Women, especially, usually receive what most Westerners would take to be very intrusive questions about their personal life, such as when the interviewee intends to start a family and in extreme cases, questions such as what kind of contraception they use. Male candidates are frequently asked whether they intend to marry in the near future, the nationality of their prospective partner, whether they have any history of mental illness or sexually transmitted diseases. These frank questions are intended to indicate how much of your private circumstances you are prepared to reveal to the company. The process has much more to do with form rather than substance and the key is not to over-react to such questioning, but to give the interviewer the kind of answers he wants to hear; that you are willing to make a long-term commitment to the company (whether or not that is strictly true) and that you do not object to the company intruding in your personal affairs.

Asking the right questions

At some stage, the person or persons who interview you will throw the ball into your court and ask if you have any questions. As the company has shown an interest in you and asked you to meet with them, it is only polite for you to show that you are as interested in their activities. Before you attend the interview, see what information you can find about the *kaisha* and think about what questions you can ask to display your interest in their business.

Being patient

Depending on the position on offer and the size and prestige of the *kaisha* considering you, you may find yourself having to attend a series of interviews before a decision is made. In some jobs, such as English teaching, one half-hour chat with the school's Director of Studies may suffice to get you your job. But with any medium or large Japanese *kaisha,* you should expect to attend three interviews (as long as both sides decide to take it that far, that is) as a minimum. There are two major reasons for this:

1. Several people will be interested to meet with you before they take the joint decision to employ you.

2. If a potential employee has enough interest to attend three, four or five interviews, this is taken as a positive sign of the person's real interest in the *kaisha*.

What to expect at the first interview

The first interview (or the first two interviews in some companies) will most likely be conducted by an officer in the company's personnel department. Don't be surprised if much of the conversation centres on your likes and dislikes, your hobbies and such. It is worth repeating that the Japanese interview process is like a betrothal. The interviewer will want to find out as much as he or she can about your character in order to decide whether you will fit into the operation. The discussion may finish without you having had the chance to talk much about your work qualifications and experience. Don't worry, this will come later.

Coming back for more

Once the personnel officer has satisfied him or herself of your suitability, the next person who will want to meet you will be the unit manager who will become your superior if and when you join the *kaisha*. More than anyone, this is the man who will make the decision about your fate. Now the questioning will become more aimed at your suitability for the job itself and about your experience and enthusiasm for the job being offered. Nevertheless, you should still be prepared for lighter discussion for the first few minutes as the manager begins the sounding out process. Again, do not be surprised if the first interview is followed by a second with the same members present.

Clearing the last hurdle

If you come through the second stage of the interview process successfully, you may be invited to yet another meeting, this time with the unit general manager, or in the case of a smaller *kaisha,* the president or one of the directors, possibly with the unit manager in attendance. By now, you should be almost home and dry. The purpose of this meeting is to acquaint you with the *kaisha's* chief executive or in the case of a large company, with the head of the department which you will be joining. The talk here should be fairly general and only intended to allow the senior man to get an idea of the character of the new employee.

Knowing the Do's and Don'ts

As well as being honest and polite, when you attend your interview, bear the following points in mind:

● Do dress according to the rules.

● Do show enthusiasm.

● Do try to be yourself and don't try to imitate what you think is Japanese behaviour. As a *gaigin,* the Japanese will expect you to be different so trying to mimic their behaviour, particularly if you do not speak their language or have only an elementary grasp, will not be to your advantage.

● Don't make jokes.

● Don't try to stare the interviewer down or push the interview in the direction you wish to take. As a potential new employee, you will be expected to follow rather than lead. Let the Japanese interviewer control the situation.

● Don't exaggerate your own achievements or abilities. The Japanese value personal modesty over confidence in one's abilities.

● Don't say you only intend to stay two or three years (even if this is really your intention). The Japanese always expect a long-term commitment and do not look favourably on potential employees who offer anything less than the same.

● Don't ask about your salary at preliminary interviews. Leave these negotiations until you have been offered a job. You will be in a stronger position (because now the *kaisha* has shown that it wants you) and to broach the subject of money early on in the process would be a breach of Japanese etiquette.

TAKING CARE OVER YOUR CONTRACT

Once you have been offered a job, you will be asked to sign a contract with the company. Typically, a contract will comprise no more than a single page and contain the basic terms and conditions of your employment. It is important that you are satisfied with the terms of employment you are being offered. You should ensure that the following conditions are included as a minimum.

1. Type of employee

Types of fulltime employment in Japanese companies can be split into two main categories, *sei-sha-in* and *shoku-taku*.

Sei-sha-in

As a *sei-sha-in,* you are considered a permanent addition to the company. *Sei-sha-in* status entitles you to not only your salary but also a twice yearly bonus. As the bonus is normally equal to two or even three times monthly earnings it is a considerable amount, although it can also decrease in line with the fortunes of the company. Salaries are organised on a scale and rise according to seniority of position, age and years of service in the company. Working as a *sei-sha-in* also means that you can be considered for promotion, an advantage denied non-*sei-sha-in* employees. Other benefits include the possibility of a subsidy for accommodation and paid transport to and from work and a lump sum on retirement, or *taishoku-kin.*

Shoku-taku

The role of a *shoku-taku* worker is basically that of a specialist brought in to do some short-term job for the *kaisha* although in the case of some workers, the short-term contract is rolled over for a number of years. As such, *shoku-taku* employees lack many of the advantages of the *sei-sha-in,* such as the payment of *taishoku-kin* on retirement and in some cases, the biannual bonus payment. Promotion is also denied *shoku-taku* workers. On the other hand, the monthly salary of a *shoku-taku* can be higher than that of a *sei-sha-in.* Other benefits, such as subsidised accommodation, vary in their availability depending on the company. If you are only considering a stay of two or three years, it could be better for you to opt for *shoku-taku* status.

Normally, the choice will be yours, though there are companies that insist on a new employee being classified as one of the two types.

Arbeito

The Japanese have borrowed the German word for work and use it to mean work that is of a part-time nature. *Arbeito* can refer to either someone employed only two or three days a week, or to someone employed to work a full working week but whose contract can be terminated with very little notice. People doing *arbeito* are usually paid an hourly rate that is better than that of *sei-sha-in* or *shoku-taku* employees but they lack any kind of job security and receive no benefits such as bonuses that are usual with a Japanese *kaisha.*

2. Salary

Like companies all over the world, most Japanese *kaisha* grade salaries according to position and years of service. As a *gaigin* joining a Japanese company, you may find that you are offered a salary commensurate with other Japanese working in the company of your age. One facet of the positive discrimination from which *gaigin* benefit is that some companies offer their foreign staff a higher salary than that of their Japanese employees. In any case, if you feel the salary you are being offered is too low, there is nothing to be lost by making a counter offer.

It is worth reminding you at this point that you are now in Japan. Remember this when you consider the remuneration on offer. While the temptation is to calculate your pay in terms of sterling or US dollars and congratulate yourself on the money you will be earning, bear in mind that the cost of living in Japan is also higher and that after accounting for this fact, your monthly salary might not appear so generous as it seemed at first glance.

The bonus system

The Japanese bonus system comes as a very pleasant surprise to most Westerners. Bonuses are usually paid twice a year, in December and July. Each bonus is calculated as a multiple of the employee's salary, with a multiple of two or three being the norm although this can change with the (improving or worsening) circumstances of the company.

3. Terms of contract

The normal term of a contract to a foreign employee is one year. This is due to the fact that most working visas granted to foreigners are also for one-year periods.

4. Overtime

Make sure that there is a condition in your contract stipulating payment for overtime. Many Japanese companies insert a clause 'allowing' a certain number of hours of overtime to be worked each month. This does not mean that you will not be allowed more overtime than the hours stipulated but it does mean you won't be paid for more overtime than the maximum in your contract. The reality for many Japanese is that their workload forces them to exceed their monthly limit and receive no pay for the extra hours worked.

5. Holidays

There should be a stipulated number of annual holidays in your contract. You should check to find out whether these 'holidays' are inclusive or exclusive of sick leave, whether the holidays are paid and whether or not there are any conditions preventing you from taking a part of your holiday allocation in one block of, say, ten days. It is important to understand that contractual holidays and the holidays you are actually allowed to take may turn out to be very different. Though things are changing, the reality is that most Japanese workers never get to take their full holiday allowance. In particular, many companies frown upon requests from workers for a number of holidays to be taken in a block.

National holidays
For a nation of reputed workaholics, Japan boasts more national holidays than most other industrialised countries. A list of dates appears in Fig. 6. Make sure you are clear whether or not the contractual holidays offered by the *kaisha* include national holidays or not.

6. Loans
Many Japanese companies make loans available to their employees, almost always at better rates than the banks and often interest free. You should check whether this facility is available to you as you may well need to consider taking out a loan with your company in order to be able to meet the costs of finding permanent accommodation.

7. Accommodation
Medium and large-sized Japanese companies invariably provide subsidised accommodation for their employees. The type of accommodation on offer can vary from a dormitory style studio with shared facilities up to a house for more senior personnel, with apartments of varying sizes in between for married couples and their children.

Other companies offer to pay a proportion of their employees' accommodation costs up to a payment ceiling which is higher or lower according to the employees' position and seniority.

8. Pensions contributions
Most larger Japanese companies make monthly payments towards their employees' government pension schemes. These payments, or *kou-sei nenkin shikin,* may be available to you. The problem is that you will not be able to claim them unless you take Japanese nationality. Therefore, it will in your best interests to ascertain whether or not your employer will be making *kou-sei nenkin shikin* contributions on your behalf, and if so, whether it is possible for you to have the payment paid as an increment to your salary rather than as a payment to the government.

1 January	New Year's Day
15 January	Adult's Day
11 February	National Foundation Day
21 March	Spring Day
29 April	Green Day
3 May	Constitution Memorial Day
5 May	Children's Day
15 September	Respect for the Aged Day
23 September	Autumnal Equinox Day
10 October	Health Day
3 November	Culture Day
23 November	Labour Day
23 December	Emperor's Birthday

Fig. 6. Calendar of Japanese National Holidays.

9. Transportation

Your new employer should offer to pay for the cost of your transport to and from your place of work.

The contract, together with its translation, in Fig. 7 shows the typical contractual terms and conditions in a medium-sized Japanese corporation for a *shoku-taku* employee.

GETTING THE RIGHT VISA

Starting work in Japan does not necessarily mean that you have to apply for a working visa. Visa conditions vary depending on the agreements your country has with Japan.

United Kingdom passport holders

Holders of a UK passport are permitted to enter Japan with only a valid passport for a visit of up to 90 days. This visa is renewable for one further 90-day period. You may not work, but if you decide to take employment, you may apply for a working visa while in Japan.

United States passport holders

Holders of a US passport may enter Japan with only a valid passport. However, tourist visas granted on entry to Japan to US citizens are not renewable, and neither can a working visa be granted within the country if the applicant holds only this visa in passport. This means that if a US passport holder finds work, he will be able to apply for a working visa within Japan, but if that application is successful, he will then have to leave Japan to receive the visa from a Japanese consulate abroad. In order to be able to apply for and receive a working visa while in Japan, US citizens should apply for a multiple-entry tourist visa to Japan prior to their visit from a Japanese consulate.

The Working Holidays Program

Citizens of Australia, Canada and New Zealand are permitted, under the terms of the program, to enter Japan on a tourist visa and work for up to twenty hours per week without the need to apply for a working visa. The tourist visa lasts for six months and can be renewed for the same period once in the case of Canadian citizens and twice in the case of Australians and New Zealanders. At the end of this period, the visa holder must change to working visa status if he or she wishes to continue working in Japan.

Applying for your working visa while in Japan

The process of applying for a working visa inside Japan is rather more complicated than the process of applying while still in your own country. One reason for this is that the process involves a *change* of visa status (from tourist visa to working visa), rather than simply an application. Secondly, you must submit the necessary documentation yourself rather than only completing the process by submitting a Certificate of Eligibility and having a working visa stamped into your passport.

Where to apply

All applications for changes to the visa status of foreign nationals must be made at a Japanese consulate.

What you need to apply for your visa

Whether your application for a working visa is made in your own country, or in Japan, the documentation required by the *homu-sho* is the

雇用契約書

(正社員 ＊ 嘱託社員 ＊ 長期パート準社員 ＊ 臨時短期パート)

株式会社 世界輸入と 　デボラー　エリス　は、以下の条件で労働契約書を締結する。

雇用期間　　1. 期間定め無し　　年　　　月　　　日より就業
　　　　　　2. 期間定め有り　6 年　8 月　17 日より　7 年　8 月　16日まで就業

就業場所　　本社 (東京都品川区1丁目38番世界輸入ビル)

仕事の内容　海外営業部営業主任

始業*終業の　午前　8 時 45 分から午後 17 時 30 分まで (休憩45 分含む)
時刻及び休憩
時間

休日　　　　日曜日,土曜日,祭日,夏期休暇,年末年始休暇　年間計 126 日

年次有給休暇　6年　8月 17日から 7年　3月 31日まで 9日。

　　　　　　1.基本給　(1)時給　(2)日給　(3)月給 (385,000 円)
　　　　　　2.諸手当　(1)住宅　　手当　　　　(55,000　円)
　　　　　　3.所定外労働に対する賃金割率
賃金等　　　　(1)残業　25%　(2)休日　25%　(3)深夜　50%
　　　　　　4.賃金締切日　　25日
　　　　　　5.賃金支給日　　5日
　　　　　　6.昇給　　　無し　　有り　但し、4月度とする。
　　　　　　7.賞与　　　無し　　有り　但し、7月度,12 月度とする。
　　　　　　8.退職金　　無し　　有り

　　　　　　1.当契約書にない事項すいては会社規定,規制による。
その他　　　2.特記事項　無し　有り

6 年　　月 17日　使用者住所　　氏名 高橋 平太
　　　　　　　　　　　　　　東京都品川区 1丁目38番 世界輸入ビル

　　　　　　　　　　労働者住所　　氏名
　　　　　　　　　　　　　　　　東京都中野区東中野 5-7-1

Fig. 7. (1 of 2) Specimen contract of employment.

Contract of Employment.

(Sei-sha-in * Shoku-taku-in * Long term part timer * Short term part timer)

The conditions below represent the employment contract made between

Kabushiki-kaisha World Imports and Ms. Deborah Ellis.

Term of Employment	1. Unlimited from
	2. From 1994/8/17 to 1995/8/17
Place of employment	Head office. (Tokyo, Shinagawa-ku. 1-chome,
	38 ban, World Import Building.)
Work content	International business department, Junior
	assistant manager.
Working hours and	From 08:45 am to 17:30 pm (Including 45 minute
rest times.	lunch break.)
Holidays	Sundays, Saturdays, National holidays, Summer
	holidays, Year end holidays, totalling 126 days.
Paid holidays	9 days from 1994/8/17 to 1995/3/31
	Salary 1.Basic salary (1)Hourly (2)Daily (3)Monthly
	(385,000 yen).
	2.Allowances (1) Accommodation.
	(55,000 yen)
	3. Payments for work outside of contract hours.
	(1) Overtime (25%) (2) Holidays (25%) (3) Late nights (50%)
	4. Working month end date: 25th of every month.
	5. Salary payment date: 5th of the following month.
	6. Salary increase: Yes No Every April.
	7. Bonus payments: Yes No July and December.
	8. Retirement benefits. Yes No
Other	1. Any items not included in this contract are subject to
	the rules and regulations of the company.
	2. Special items. Yes No
Signed as of	Employer _____.
	Employee _____.

Fig. 7. (2 of 2) Specimen contract of employment translation.

same in both cases. Refer back to the section on renewing a working visa to see exactly what you need to make an application. (See Chapter 3.)

What you get
You will receive a visa, normally for a period of one year, although some people still only receive visas for six months with no explanation offered and none given if asked for, excepting a dubious assurance that once you have been in Japan for one year (you will have to renew your six month visa) you will henceforth be granted a one-year visa. Sometimes this is proved to be the case, at other times, the unlucky applicant still finds himself with a six-month visa even after completing his first year in Japan. In this case, the only recourse is to do as the Japanese do and *gaman suru*, or grin and bear it.

Normally you will have to wait two or three weeks from the time when you submit your application. You will receive a postcard telling you to return to the *homu-sho* to get the visa stamped into your passport, or alternatively asking you to return to answer any further queries the *homu-sho* officials might have. (Don't worry unduly. As long as you are working for a bona fide company, you should have no problems.)

Renewing your visa

Working visa renewals are done in exactly the same way as for those who receive their working visa outside Japan. (See Chapter 3.)

Changing employers

Changing employers necessitates another trip to the *homu-sho* and the submission of further documentation as listed below:

- letter of resignation
- statement of reasons for resignation
- your new employment contract
- statement of reasons for employment
- letter of guarantee from your new employer
- the same company documents as were submitted at the time of your original application.

Changing status

There are a total of 18 varieties of Japanese residence visa. A breakdown of the details of the types of visa is shown in Fig. 8. It may be that if you change from one type of employment to another, you may also have to apply for a different class of visa. This is certainly true of foreign nationals marrying Japanese citizens who after marriage have to change their working visa to a spouse visa. The details concerning changes from

Status of residence	Qualifying persons	Period of stay
4-1-1	Diplomats and consular officials accredited to Japan and their families	During mission
4-1-2	Officials of foreign governments or international organisations recognised by the Japanese government and their families	During mission
4-1-4	Temporary visitors with the following plans; travel, sports activities, visit relatives, inspection tours, participate in meetings or short courses, attend business meetings	90 days, 60 days, 30 days or 15 days
4-1-5	Persons engaging in management of business, foreign trade, or capital investment activities	3 years, 1 year, 6 or 3 months
4-1-6	Students engaging in study or research at the junior college level or above	1 year, 6 or 3 months
4-1-6-2	Persons accepted by a public or private organisation in Japan to acquire industrial techniques or skills	1 year, 6 or 3 months
4-1-7	Lecturers and professors engaging in full-time teaching at educational or research institutions	3 years, 1 year, 6 or 3 months
4-1-8	Persons engaging in activities with a high level in the arts and sciences (music, fine arts, literature, etc.)	1 year, 6 or 3 months
4-1-9	Paid entertainers such as singers, actors, professional athletes, their managers and entourage	60 days, 30 days or 15 days
4-1-10	Persons dispatched to Japan by foreign religious organisations to conduct religious activities (including non-paid educational or medical activities)	3years , 1 year, 6 or 3 months
4-1-11	Persons dispatched to Japan for news gathering purposes by foreign newspapers, radio and TV broadcasters and other journalistic organisations (excluding freelancers)	3 years, 1 year, 6 or 3 months
4-1-12	Persons invited by public or private organisations in Japan for the purpose of furnishing high level or specialised skills and know how	3 years, 1 year, 6 or 3 months
4-1-13	Persons engaged in skilled labour (e.g. cooks in Chinese or French restaurants, Western style confectioners, etc.)	1 year, 6 or 3 months
4-1-14	Persons seeking to reside permanently in Japan	Permanent
4-1-15	Spouses and unmarried minor children of any person coming under status 4-1-5 through 4-1-13 above (excluding minor children who are college students, employed or otherwise engaged in any activity which falls under another residence status category)	Same as supporting spouse or parent
4-1-16-1	Spouses or children of any Japanese national (if residing in Japan as family members of Japanese nationals)	3 years, 1 year, 6 or 3 months
4-1-16-2	Children whose Korean or Taiwanese parent has been living in Japan since before the end of the Second World War or since birth if born after 28 April 1952	3 years
4-1-16-3	Persons who do not fall under any other status but are permitted to reside at the discretion of the Minister of Justice (under this status medical doctors, teachers at foreign language schools, dependents of Japanese nationals, etc. are permitted to enter and stay)	3 years, 1 year, 6 or 3 months

Fig. 8. Types of Japanese residence visa.

one sort of visa to another change quite frequently so it is best that if you change jobs during your stay in Japan, you contact your nearest *homu-sho* to receive guidance on your position.

After receiving your working visa

Just as if you had received your working visa outside Japan, it is now your responsibility to register your residence at your city office, *shiyaku-sho*, or ward office, *kuyaku-sho*. The same regulations apply: you must apply for your *gaigin* card within 90 days of receiving your working visa and you must *always* carry the card on your person.

RE-ENTRY PERMITS

When you return to the *homu-sho* to have your passport stamped with your new working visa, take the opportunity to apply for a multiple re-entry permit, which you will need in order to be able to travel freely to and from Japan during the period of your residence.

5
Managing your Budget

TRAVELLING AND LIVING COSTS

The budget in Fig. 9. lists your likely costs for a four-week stay in Japan while you are looking for your job. You should bear in mind that these costs are calculated for those on tight budget so the accommodation will be basic, either a *gaigin* house accommodating only foreign guests, or a youth hostel. The air fare budget is for tourist class on one of the less popular international carriers.

Minimum budget for return airfare to Japan and a month stay	
Airfare (return, one year open if budget allows)	£ 600 - 850
Accommodation for four weeks (28 days)	£ 400 - 450
Food and drink	£ 350 - 400
Travel to interviews, telephone calls, etc.	£ 300 - 400
Miscellaneous expenses	£ 350 - 400
	£2000-2500

Fig. 9. Budgeting for a trip to Japan.

Choosing an airfare

Airfares to Japan vary considerably depending on the airline you travel with, the time you choose to travel and the route you choose to take. Generally speaking, February and early March and late October to November are the slackest times on the direct London-Tokyo route which also means that the most attractive fares will be on offer. If you wish to keep yourself to as tight as budget as possible, steer clear of the flag carriers, BA and Japan Airlines. Virgin Atlantic and All Nippon Airlines offer slightly more economic fares. The cheapest prices of all on the direct route are available from the Russian airline, Aeroflot.

Taking the southern route

A cheaper alternative to the above airlines exists in the form of the southern route. As the name suggests, this involves flying on a Middle Eastern or Asian airline, first to the carrier's home destination and then, normally after a change of aircraft, onwards to Japan. Examples of airlines operating on the souther routes are:

Pakistan International Airlines:	Flies from London to Tokyo via Karachi.
Air India:	Flies from London to Tokyo via New Delhi.
Cathay Pacific:	Flies from London to Tokyo via Hong Kong.

Note that these airlines may also make further stops en route. Check with your travel agent.

Choosing a ticket

Return airfares almost always work out cheaper than two singles. As a rule you would be wise to buy a return as a precaution against your failing to find a job in Japan. Possibly the best ticket to get is one that has the return portion open for as long as possible. Although more expensive, you might consider buying a ticket with the return portion open for one year. That way, once you are settled into Japan, you will be able to return to the UK during a holiday, both to visit and also to pick up all those bits and pieces you wish you had taken with you when you first went out to Japan. It is probably not necessary to mention that discount fare shops offer better ticketing deals than those available at high street agents and airline booking offices.

Sorting out your accommodation

Unless you can afford a much bigger budget than the one above, accommodation in city hotels, or their traditional Japanese counterpart, the *ryokan*, is going to be out of your reach financially. Most foreigners arriving in Japan in search of work normally take one of two options.

1. *Gaigin houses*

Gaigin houses, guest houses for foreigners, are found in all of the bigger cities in Japan, normally in the cheaper areas. Typical cost for a room and shared facilities with no meals is 2,000-2,500 yen per night (£12-15 at current rates of exchange).

Pros

- good place to meet other foreigners and start networking
- international atmosphere means less chance of feeling alienated
- cheap

Cons

- can be noisy at times
- some reports of theft at some *gaigin* houses
- most *gaigin* houses do not take reservations.

2. *Japanese Youth Hostels*

There are over 450 Japanese Youth Hostels and you will find them in all of Japan's major centres. Accommodation is shared in dormitories, normally of eight beds. Costs are around 1,500-2,000 yen per night (£9-12 at current rates of exchange). Furthermore, very economical meals are available at about £4. You may need to provide evidence of membership to the IYH organisation so you would be well advised to join before leaving for Japan if you intend to stay in a youth hostel. Alternatively, you can become a member once you have arrived in Japan for a fee of approximately £9. The address of the Japan Youth Hostels Association can be found in the Appendix.

Pros

- clean and well managed
- normally very close to the city centre
- staff are helpful and can be valuable source of information.

Cons

- shared accommodation
- you may have to do some light housework in the mornings.

Alternatives

If you feel that neither of the above is for you, then the only other option which is not prohibitively expensive is the business hotel. As the name suggests, these hotels are aimed at businessmen travelling around Japan on a budget. There are literally hundreds of these establishments in every city. Prices at the bottom of the range are from 4,000 yen per night (£24 at current rates of exchange.)

A comprehensive list of *gaigin* houses and youth hostels in the major Japanese centres is included in the Appendix of this book. You should also visit or telephone the Japan National Tourist Office before you leave and ask for a copy of their lists of low-priced hotels before your departure.

Eating on a budget in Japan

After all the tales you have heard about the sky-high costs of living in Japan, eating out in Tokyo, Osaka or anywhere in Japan, comes as a pleasant surprise. Contrary to what you have read and heard, it is possible to eat three good, wholesome meals on a budget of around £15 per day.

Where to go

Small cafes or *kissa-ten* abound all over Japan. Times vary, but normally a breakfast set menu of (real) coffee, toast and butter is offered until 10.00 a.m. Cost is around 450-500 yen.

For lunch, you should try either a noodle shop, or *ramen-ya*, or alternatively, one of the many small and economical Chinese restaurants or *chuka-ryori-ya*, that can be found in every Japanese city and town. Both of these eating places display the dishes available in plastic form in the display window so you can choose whatever takes your eye. Prices vary according to the dish chosen, but you should be able to eat your fill for 750 yen both at midday and in the evening.

If you find yourself needing something a little closer to what you are used to at home, you will be able to find a MacDonalds, Kentucky Fried Chicken or Wimpy Burger in any of the big cities or towns at prices not much different from those charged in the UK.

Eating places to avoid

- **Hotel restaurants**: the prices here are oriented towards expense account holders. You could find yourself spending a week's food allowance for one evening meal.

- **Any restaurant serving European or Indian cuisine**: as European and Indian restaurants are fashionable places to eat, prices are accordingly high.

- **Sushi bars**: it would be a shame to spend time in Japan without sampling Japanese *sushi* and *sashimi*. Some bars serving this cuisine are very reasonably priced but the bill does tend to get expensive nevertheless. You would be better to wait until you are fixed up with a job before splashing out.

Telephone calls and cost of travel

The telephone and the train are your two indispensable tools for finding a job in Japan. Fortunately, both are hardly more expensive than in the UK and in the case of the trains, the standard of service is incomparably better and more reliable than what you are used to.

The railway system in Japan is a combination of privately run lines, such as the Keio Line and the Seibu Line, together with the quasi-privatised national network that is Japan Railways, or JR, as it has been known since privatisation. The city networks are extensive and tickets bought and used on one private line can be used to travel on another private line or on Japan Railways if a change of trains is necessary to get to your destination. The system does take some getting used to but almost all stations on both the subway and the overground lines display maps of the system in English so even if you do lose your way, you should have no trouble getting back on the right track again. The Japanese National Tourist Office will be happy to supply you with underground maps prior to your trip.

PREPARING FOR YOUR TRIP

To give your job hunt in Japan the maximum chance of success, you should make careful preparations before your journey.

Arranging your finances

As calculated above, you should consider having at least £2,000 at your disposal.

Renewing your passport

As long as your passport (which must be of either five or ten year type) has at least six months left prior to expiry and two clean pages (one for your tourist visa and another for your working visa when it is granted), you should not need to renew your passport before your trip. Passports can be renewed at the British Embassy once you are in Japan.

UK passport holders need only to present their passport on arrival in Japan to get a renewable three-month tourist visa. US passport holders should apply in the USA for a multiple entry tourist visa. Australians, Canadians and New Zealanders should apply for participation in the Working Holidays programme.

Gathering information and documents

There are a number of sources of useful information that you should use before making the trip to Japan. Among the best are:

- The Japanese consulate for general information about Japan and information on visa formalities.
- The Japanese National Tourist Organisation for street maps and information about budget hotels, restaurants as well as more general information.

Taking out an International Driver's Licence

This is something worth considering if you intend to drive while you are in Japan. Alternatively, it is possible to get a Japanese licence once you are living in Japan as long as you have held a driving licence for more than three months.

Applying for membership of the Youth Hostel Organisation

This will be necessary if you intend to stay at a youth hostel at any time after your arrival in Japan. Alternatively, you can apply after arrival in Japan.

Making reservations

You will need to purchase your airline ticket. You should also make forward reservations for accommodation in Japan, if this is possible.

Buying clothing

It is important that your clothes are clean and free of visible signs of wear. You should therefore think about whether it is necessary to buy some new items of clothing for your trip. As you will not want to be burdened with clothing to suit all the seasons, take only what you will need for the next six months. Once you are settled into your new life, you can arrange for other clothing to be sent to you by sea mail.

Buying traveller's cheques

Notwithstanding the fact that Japan is one of the safest countries on earth, it would still not be wise to carry large amounts of cash around with you. Traveller's cheques are far safer. You should consider whether it is best to purchase TCs in your local currency or in Japanese yen. Credit cards are another option if you wish to keep funds back in the UK. As your spending in Japan will be in Japanese yen, you should check that your card issuer offers competitive rates of exchange. Whichever option you choose, you should also exchange about £100 for yen before your journey.

Electrical appliances

Electrical supply in Japan is rated at 100 volts. Consequently, no European applicance will work in Japan. Buying a small universal transformer will meet most of your immediate needs, such as razors and radios. For larger equipment, a larger, more expensive converter is necessary. These can cost £75-100 and weigh up to 10 kg, or half of your flight baggage allowance. As you can imagine, you would be better off buying a Japanese rated applicance once you have arrived in Japan.

ARRIVING IN JAPAN

The chances are that you will arrive in Japan at the country's main airport, Tokyo International at Narita, although there is the possibility that you will enter via Osaka International, particularly if you have decided to stop-over en route in South East Asia.

Arriving at Narita

The title 'Tokyo International Airport' is misleading as Narita is in fact located in the centre of Chiba Prefecture, 30 miles east of Tokyo. When you have passed through the immigration and customs formalities, you will find a bureau de change immediately behind the customs counters if you have not yet changed any money into yen. Leaving the customs area, you will find yourself in the arrivals lobby. There are several banks of telephones here, so if you need to make arrangements for accommodation, now is the time to do it. Even if you have already made your reservation, it might be worth telephoning to ask the name of the nearest station if you don't already know this. Once you are ready to leave the airport, there are several options for getting away.

Narita Express

Part of Japan Railways, the Narita Express shuttle is the fastest and most convenient way to get from the airport to central Tokyo. The trains leave from underneath the airport, are well signposted and are accessed by escalator from the arrivals lobby. There are two drawbacks to the Narita Express service:

● The trains only run between two and three times an hour and consequently sell out very quickly. Tickets for the services can be bought from machines in the first floor basement if available. If the next service is already sold out, this information will be flashed up on the ticketing machine display. You cannot board any Narita Express train without a ticket and no standing on board is permitted.

- The Narita Express service is fairly expensive. Single fares from Narita airport to Tokyo Station cost 3,000 yen, or roughly £18. If your budget does not allow you to consider this kind of expense, it would be wiser for you to consider the next alternative.

Other Japan Railways services

JR always runs regular scheduled services on the Sotobo line between Narita Airport and Tokyo station and beyond to Yokohama, depending on the service. These trains run between once and twice an hour. As the train is a stopping service or *kaku-eki-tesha*, the trip to Tokyo lasts about an hour and thirty minutes, but this does provide a very interesting introduction to Japan. On the positive side, the fare, at 1,260 yen or £7.50, is one of the cheapest ways of getting into Tokyo and there is never any problem getting aboard. Also, as the train stops at several other stations in Tokyo, it may bring you closer to your accommodation. Tickets for the Sotobo line service are available from machines in the first basement level on the left of the machines for the Narita Express.

These trains often include carriages called 'Green cars'. The seats in these carriages are more expensive than those in the normal carriages and you will be charge an excess fare if an inspector finds you in a Green car seat with only a standard ticket. Green car carriages are clearly labelled, so make sure not to sit in one by mistake.

Keisei Line

The private Keisei line also runs an express service, the Skyliner, between Narita Airport and Ueno station in the northern part of Tokyo, the trip taking just over an hour. The service is frequent and at 1,740 yen, or £10, also economical.

Other Keisei Line services

Scheduled railway services are also available on the Keisei line from the same location. These services are slower than the Skyliner, taking more than an hour and a half, but this is reflected in the lower price of 940 yen.

The Narita Airport Limousine Bus service

Services run once an hour and twice an hour at peak times. Ticket counters can be found in the arrivals lobby and the staff speak English. The advantage of the limousine bus is that it stops near several of the main hotel centres in Tokyo and therefore may drop you closer to your accommodation than the train would do. The drawbacks are:

- The limousine bus is as expensive as the Narita Express.

- Depending on the traffic encountered on the way up from the airport, the bus can take anything from an hour to two and a half hours to reach the centre of Tokyo.

Taxis
This is the most expensive option of all. Very few people, least of all *gaigin*, use the taxis that run between the airport and Tokyo. Charges of £150-200 are not unusual.

Arriving at Osaka
If you are coming from South East Asia, or if you are travelling to a job in Osaka or western Japan, you may choose Osaka International Airport as your point of arrival rather than Narita. Happily, Osaka International is a lot closer to the city than Narita to Tokyo. Transport options are as follows:

- Osaka Airport Limousine Bus
- Hanshin Limousine Bus

These two limousine bus services to downtown Osaka leave the airport six to eight times an hour, the trip taking from 25 to 40 minutes depending on the destination within Osaka and unless the traffic is heavy. The one-way fare costs only 510 yen or around £3.

Keeping in touch
Once you have arrived in Japan, make a short call home to assure everyone that you have arrived safely and, more importantly, to give them details of where you are staying.

Your second call should be to the British Embassy to inform them of your arrival and whereabouts. You may never have cause to contact the people there again during your stay, but remember that in cases of emergency, they could (literally) save your life.

6
Job Opportunities for Foreigners in Japan

The following list of jobs is a representative selection of the kind of opportunities you should find in Japan together with information about requirements, conditions and levels of pay you can expect. At the end of the chapter (Fig. 10) two pages of jobs are printed from the classified section of a single Monday edition of the *Japan Times*, Japan's top selling English language daily. This should give you some idea of the variety of positions available.

Accounting

The globalisation of Japanese business and the increasing number of companies establishing subsidiaries and branch operations in Japan has created significant opportunities for accountants in Japan. Japanese companies require accounting experience in the foreign tax jurisdictions where their overseas operations are based while foreign companies in Japan need accountants able to financially integrate their operations in Japan with those of their parent company. For non-certified accounting staff, a number of posts are usually available through agencies and the press both in Japanese and foreign companies.

Availability	**
Location	Typically Tokyo, Osaka and Kobe.
Requirements	Certified accountants need to have several years of experience to offer, often in a related multi-jurisdiction environment. Non-certified accounting staff should normally possess some relevant qualifications as well as experience.
Pay	750,000 + yen plus benefits, especially for those working on an expatriate package. 250,000 + yen for accounting staff plus benefits, though non-certified staff almost always hired locally.

Advertising/Copywriting

Opportunities do exist for foreigners within the world of Japanese advertising although they occur more rarely now than several years ago when some knowledge of Japanese was enough to get a young foreigner hired by a major agency. At present, the vacancies that arise usually require experience with a major foreign advertising agency and Japanese language ability, while preferred, is not essential.

Availability	*
Location	Mostly Tokyo.
Requirements	Most Japanese advertising companies now require at least three to four years prior experience.
Pay	400,000 yen + and benefits, bigger salaries for those recruited from abroad.

Architecture

Japanese architecture ranks amongst the most creative and avant garde in the world. Modern Japanese designs have been heavily influenced by European and American architecture and consequently, many Japanese design offices and large construction firms with their own teams of in-house designers have shown a willingness to hire foreign creative talent. Most openings tend to be in the unadvertised market, meaning that foreign architects need in most cases to make the first approach. As yet, the numbers of foreign architects making a living in Japan is not high, but this is probably more a reflection on the number of architects coming to Japan to look for work, rather than the reluctance of Japanese companies to employ them.

Availability	**
Location	Tokyo and Osaka for the major firms. Smaller companies can be found in other major cities.
Requirements	The same as would be required as in the architect's country of origin. Japanese language ability is also clearly an advantage.
Pay	500,000 yen + but depends very much on experience, reputation and the company involved.

Banking and finance

Opportunities for foreigners in Japanese banking and finance exploded as Japan's banks and financial institutions expanded their overseas operations dramatically during the 1980s. The benefit of hindsight shows that this expansion was, if anything, too sudden and these operations have since been subject to retrenchment. It was not unusual during the 1980s for foreigners with a grasp of Japanese and no prior experience in finance to find jobs working for Japanese banks and stockbrokers. The situation in the 1990s is much changed and the ability to speak Japanese is no longer the passport to a well-paid job. The Japanese now recruit almost exclusively from the ranks of those with several years experience, concentrating their recruitment on individuals who can bring a skill in a particular field of finance with them.

Availability	**
Location	Almost exclusively Tokyo and to a lesser extent Osaka.
Requirements	Japanese language ability is a plus but no means essential. The emphasis has changed to hiring foreigners who have experience in an area where local talent is not available. Education usually required at least to MA level and often beyond.
Pay	From 500,000 yen monthly + bonus, benefits.

Computers

The Japanese have succeeded in developing a very strong domestic computer hardware industry and boasts some of the world's most technologically developed systems. This success has not been matched by similar advances in the software industry which is still dominated by US makers. Some say that the Japanese education does not produce minds creative enough to develop sophisticated software packages. Whether or not this is true, it has created opportunities for foreigners to lend their expertise. Most of the major Japanese hardware manufacturers and their subsidiaries recruit foreign staff for their research programmes as do some of the smaller software houses. Other job openings exist, in both Japanese and foreign finance houses in systems engineering and programming.

Availability	***
Location	Mostly in Tokyo and Osaka though R&D work exists in other regions.
Requirements	Education to BsC level is a must and normally further qualifications required, as is proof of occupational experience and ability.
Pay	650,000 + salary with good systems engineers earning much more.

Disc jockeying

A small but lucrative market exists in Tokyo, Osaka and other large Japanese cities for foreign DJs. Most things Western possess an allure for the Japanese and many discotheques like to boast a foreign disc jockey to give themselves more appeal to the young, image conscious Japanese. Experience is necessary and applicants will normally be required to give a demonstration of their ability before being offered any work.

Availability	*
Location	Major cities.
Requirements	Experience, but most important is a good mock session.
Pay	50,000 + yen per night.

English teaching

English teaching is the most widely available source of work for foreigners in Japan. The Japanese have an appetite for learning the language both for business and for pleasure and the demand for teachers continues to exceed the supply of foreigners available to fill the positions. Many people use English teaching as a stop gap while they get settled into Japan and source other work, while others are happy to concentrate on what is a fairly undemanding way of earning a living. For those who see English teaching as a career rather than as a means to an end, attractive long-term opportunities exist at Japanese senior colleges and universities where English is studied at degree level.

Availability	*****
Location	All over Japan, though best paying positions are in the cities.
Requirement	Teaching certificates and experience required varies from school to school. All schools do demand teachers to have been educated to at least university level, however.
Pay	200,000 + yen salary with considerably more for those with jobs at the top schools and universities and lucrative part-time work on the side.

Hostessing

Working as a hostess in one of Japan's ubiquitous hostess bars or night clubs falls under the umbrella of jobs which the Japanese call the 'water trade' or *mizu-shobai*. Working as a hostess carries a lot of negative connotations due to foreign misunderstanding as to the nature of the work. Hostessing in Japan is most definitely not a euphemistic term for prostitution. Instead, the work mostly involves making small talk with the members of the bar or club, serving their drinks and lighting their cigarettes. Cases of hostesses being forced into prostitution, sad though they are, always involve women from South East Asia, although you would be wise to check out any bar or club before going to work there. Working hours are usually from 6.00 p.m. until 1.00 or 2.00 a.m. four or five days per week. One potential problem involves visas as the Ministry of Justice will most likely not grant a working visa for this occupation. To avoid this problem, the best idea is to get your work visa via another occupation, for example teaching English. Doing this part-time in the afternoon, two or three days a week will then leave you with time to work as a hostess in the evening as well as solving the visa issue.

Availability	***
Location	All over Japan but the clubs wanting to hire foreign staff will most likely be in Tokyo and Osaka.
Requirements	Appearance and personality are the most important factors. Some Japanese ability is an advantage, though in most cases not essential as many of the bar's clients will want to converse in English.
Pay	200,000 + yen per month, more in the best clubs in areas such as the Ginza and Akasaka.

Law

As Japan's international activities have increased over the last fifteen years, so has the need for foreign legal expertise. This in turn, has led to two developments. First, the number of foreign law firms opening offices in Tokyo has increased and second, Japanese law firms, or *bengoshi jimu-sho*, have increased their hiring of foreign lawyers as 'trainer' staff. The reason for foreign lawyers being titled trainees, simply put, is that foreigner lawyers are barred from practising law in Japan unless they have worked for five years or more in a jurisdiction that grants equal rights to Japanese lawyers as are granted to the lawyer working in Japan. In cases where a lawyer can meet those conditions, they can apply for a licence to become a *gaikoku jimu bengoshi*, meaning a lawyer allowed to practise foreign law in Japan. Many lawyers, particularly from the USA are unable to meet these conditions and are therefore hired as trainees. These young lawyers are usually called upon to do the research work and liaison work with foreign law firms, while the Japanese lawyers in the firm they work for do the actual business with their Japanese clients.

Availability   **

Location   Tokyo, Osaka, Kobe, in that order.

Requirements   The Japanese look for practising lawyers, particularly those specialising in areas where the Japanese law firm needs foreign expertise.

Pay   1,000,000 + yen monthly and higher plus benefits.

Modelling

A common misconception amongst the foreign community in Japan goes that any white-skinned Caucasian can pick up work as a model. While it is true that many young Western women do pick up spare cash from doing occasional photo sessions or eventing at trade shows and the like, the reality is that most Japanese model agencies require experienced models with a portfolio of prior work done in their own country. The biggest agencies almost always demand 'tear sheets', that is pages taken from magazines, as this proves the model has actually done work, rather than just paid for a photographer to shoot a portfolio of pictures. Unless the model has a big reputation, developing work in Japan will take time as he or she develops *kone* amongst the model agencies. Consequently, many foreign models find part-time work to tide them over while they are getting started in the Japanese modelling business. Anyone thinking of trying to find modelling work in Japan should first of all look at the kind of 'look' Japanese agencies want in their foreign models as this is quite often very different from what is considered desirable by an agency in London or New York.

Availability   **

Location   Most agencies have their offices in Tokyo.

Requirements   A big reputation and proof of work for top foreign agencies is the quickest way to work. Failing this, a good portfolio is essential.

Pay   500,000 + per day for established models. 40,000 + per day for eventing and lower level modelling.

Music

There are opportunities in Japan within the music industry, both performing and recording, but like modelling, the money earned from these pursuits is best thought of as pocket money rather than as a sole means of making a living in Japan. It is certainly true that Western music of all sorts is hugely popular in Japan, especially with the younger generations, and big international stars find the country a very lucrative destination on their world tour itineraries. The situation for foreigners living in Japan, however, even those who may have considerable experience and can muster a list of famous musicians with whom they have performed, is very different, and even playing as back up for leading Japanese musicians does not earn the majority of foreign musicians enough money to make music their sole occupation. Most musicians actively performing do so at clubs and other small venues on an irregular basis, and these 'one nighters' don't normally earn more than 10,000-12,000 yen in fees.

Another source of part-time work can be found writing music with earnings of 60,000-75,000 per song possible. Again, such work is likely to be intermittent and only available to those who have spent the considerable time necessary to build up their network or *kone* within the Japanese music industry.

Availability	*
Location	Performances can take place anywhere but most work is likely to be found in the bigger cities. Song-writing work will inevitably be found in Tokyo.
Requirements	Performers who are looking to play back up need to have already developed a reputation in the same role somewhere abroad. Those wishing to play at smaller venues may find themselves being given an evening's work on the basis of a demo tape. Writers really need solid connections in the recording industry more than anything else to pick up work.
Pay	Song-writing up to 100,000 yen per song. Performing 100,000 yen + per event for backing a recognised Japanese artist, as little as 10,000 yen for performing at a small venue.

Retailing

During the last five or six years, major Japanese department stores have begun hiring foreign employees to fulfil certain roles in their operations. First and foremost, foreigners have been hired as floor staff to assist foreign shoppers. Positions also exist in purchasing and export departments where foreign language ability forms an important part of the job.

Availability	**
Location	Tokyo, Osaka.
Requirements	Japanese language ability, experience of retailing

	environment an advantage.
Pay	250,000 yen + benefits.

Science

The Japanese are regarded as a nation of innovators rather than inventors so it comes as a surprise to many that a huge amount of scientific research is carried out in Japanese universities and companies and furthermore, that the Japanese enthusiastically welcome the participation of foreign researchers in their research facilities. The numbers of scholarships offered by government institutions is relatively small. The Japanese Society for the Promotion of Science offers fifty post-doctoral research fellowships annually, while the Japanese Science and Technology Agency offers support to fifty young foreign researchers. As always, it is the private sector business where the real opportunities are to be found and the demand for foreign scientific participation is so great that demand has always outstripped the supply of researchers coming to carry out their work in Japan. Research positions in Japanese companies are available across a broad spectrum of industry classifications from heavy industry to pharmaceuticals to food and drink.

Availability	***
Location	Research facilities are distributed throughout Japan.
Requirements	Post-graduate qualifications and prior research experience. Japanese language ability is not usually a requirement but is clearly an advantage in carrying out research.
Pay	Scholarships plus support for accommodation and air fares.

Secretaries/personal assistants

Experienced foreign secretaries, particularly those with Japanese language ability are in steady demand in Japan, if only because of their rarity. The Japanese have little conception of the role of a Western style secretary, primarily because they do not exist as such in Japanese companies. Consequently, many foreign executives find that Japanese personnel do not meet their needs in this respect, particularly when they are looking for a secretary who can organise and take on a considerable amount of responsibility.

Availability	**
Location	Tokyo, Osaka.

Requirements	Experience and the usual secretarial skills, such as shorthand, WP, etc.
Pay	300,000 yen + plus benefits.

Sports coaching

The Japanese work and play hard. Sports are taken seriously and the average Japanese uses more of his leisure time to 'practise' rather than simply enjoy the physical and social benefits of participation. As a result, plenty of opportunities exist for coaching work in sports such as golf, tennis and skiing. Being taught by a competent foreigner is attractive to many as the Japanese tend to view themselves as inferior in sporting terms to Americans and Europeans and therefore see a foreign coach as a way of improving their ability. As with sports coaching anywhere, the nature of the work makes it seasonal rather than a full-time occupation. Many Japanese also like to combine coaching with an opportunity to polish up on their English, giving English native speakers another advantage over their Japanese counterparts. As well as coaching in the accepted sense, many openings exist in the cities for positions such as aerobics and dance instructors.

Availability	***
Location	Golf, skiing, scuba tend to be limited to resort areas. Tennis, aerobics instructing, etc. is more likely to be found in the cities.
Requirements	Prior experience is always a strong selling point although some employers will take on coaches /instructors after a satisfactory demonstration of their skill.
Pay	3,000-5,000 yen per hour basic, far more if the coach, instructor is well established in his/her field.

Trading

The biggest Japanese trading houses, such as C. Itoh and Mitsui, possess enormous power in Japan and also command a worldwide presence. As trading, and to a growing degree, finance, form the greatest part of their activities, all the trading houses are developing a growing need for foreign personnel both to assist with their operations and in certain cases to take a leading role in areas where the trading house wishes to develop new business but lacks the requisite expertise in-house. The trading houses often employ young foreign graduates as 'freshmen' or inexperienced recruits whom they can train along with their intake of Japanese graduates.

Availability   **

Location   Principally Tokyo and Osaka.

Requirements   A good degree from a top university for 'freshmen'. For experienced workers, post-graduate qualifications as well as specialist experience and skill in an area where the trading house lacks expertise.

Pay   Freshmen 250,000 yen + benefits. Can be many times higher for experienced professionals.

Translating

Not all foreigners see Japan's high trade surplus with the rest of the world as a threat. Almost every manufactured good Japan export is accompanied by some literature describing the products function and use. With the growing complexity of manufactured goods, particularly electronics, these translations must be both exact and easy to comprehend. This has lead to a growing amount of translation work being done by foreigners resident in Japan rather than native Japanese. A number of large translating companies exist offering services such as simultaneous interpreting at conferences as well as translation of written texts. Most of these companies distribute their work to a large pool of freelance or part-time translators, keeping the number of full-time employees to a minimum. This suits most translators as well, as it gives them the opportunity to work for more than one company and also to develop work direct to the client rather than having to use a middle man. Usually, a translator will work for one or two companies while they get their own client base established and then concentrate more and more exclusively on developing their own customer base. As most translating companies charge for services by the page (anything from 3,000 yen +) but pay translators by the hour (from 2,500 +), it is easy to understand why translators prefer to work for themselves rather than for a company.

Availability   ***

Locations   Freelance workers can base themselves anywhere if they have access to a telephone and fax.

Requirements   Some companies look for prior experience and qualifications but usually a demonstration of one's skills is sufficient to secure work.

Travel consulting

The increasing number of foreigners living in Japan during the 1980s coincided with a huge increase in the number of Japanese travelling overseas for their holidays. Traditionally, airline ticketing in Japan had

QUALIFIED ACCOUNTANTS/CONTROLLERS urgently required for the following positions. Please call Oaks International 0120-094145 or 03-3561-6411 for more information (Authorization No. 13 Ko0176, 9:30 a.m.-6:30 p.m).

1. ACCOUNTING Manager for worldwide consulting firm. Age under 45.

2. ASSISTANT Accounting Manager for U.S. computer manufacturer. Age under 30.

3. CHIEF Accountant for Japanese fine chemical manufacturer. Age under 35.

4. ACCOUNTANT for U.S. mechanical firm. Age 25-35.

5. ACCOUNTANT for Australian Bank. Age under 30.

6. ACCOUNTANT or Auditor for major Japanese housing firm. Age 28-42.

7. CONTROLLER for major U.S. distributor. Age 37-43.

8. ACCOUNTING Manager for European food importer. Age under 35.

EUROPEAN RESTAURANT in Gotanda requires active day waitress. No Japanese language necessary. Proper visa required. Please call Mr. Alfred 03-3442-3668, 3 Linden.

RESTAURANT WAITRESS wanted at VIVA ETHNIC. Young foreign female with proper visa who can speak some Japanese and enjoys music. South American welcome. Mon.-Fri. 7:00 p.m.-11:00 p.m. We pay ¥2,000 per hour plus transportation fee. For interview call (03) 3643-3333 after 1:00 p.m. from Monzennakacho station on Tozai Line.

TEMPORARY STAFF WANTED

Assistant to person making ad presentations to clients, and interacting with clients and the media.

Qualifications: Native female speaker of English, well-versed in Japanese, age between 20-30.
Working place: Dentsu headquarters at its Presentation Center.
Working hours: 9:30 a.m. — 17:30 p.m.
Remuneration: ¥300,000 per month, complete social benefits, paid holidays.
Application: Upon telephone notification, bring your resume with photo, in person.

100% subsidiary of Dentsu Inc.

DENTSU ECHO INC.
Dentsu Kosan Daini Bldg. 2F
1-7-13, Tsukiji, Chuo-ku, Tokyo 104
Tel: 03 (3544) 9621 License: (HAN: 13-01-0112)

WORLD-WIDE Organization looking for young, aggressive Marketing Director in motivation field. Good income, good future. Age up to 45. Send resume to: LMI Japan, 101, 3-10-14, Ebisu-Minami, Shibuya-ku, Tokyo 〒150.

HOSTESSES 7 p.m.-2 a.m. Details at interview. Respectable members' club nearby Akasaka-mitsuke Stn. Decent standards. Proper visa required. Call after 6 p.m., 03-3584-3720 or 03-3586-7568. Verdor.

BLOOMBERG BUSINESS NEWS, a 24-hour global news service, needs energetic staff for the following positions:

EARNINGS EDITOR. Good analytic and spreadsheet skills and sound knowledge of financial markets. Will analyze company earning reports.

RADIO/TV CORRESPONDENT. Broadcast journalist experience, good interviewing and management skills. Will establish and manage radio and television programs focusing on current financial news and financial news makers.

MARKET REPORTER. Bilingual print journalist to write English articles. Will cover broad range of local financial news.

Exceptional opportunities in a rapidly growing and dynamic work environment. Call OAK Associates, business consultants, at (03) 3760-8451.

TRANSLATION COMPANY SEEKS experienced female native English rewriter. Requirements: Fluent in spoken Japanese, computer Macintosh experience (MSWord). Working hours: 9:30-17:30 (Mon.-Fri.). Salary ¥17,500/day. Telephone to set interview or Fax resume in English, plus photo and copy of visa status. Kokusai Koryu Center. Tel: 03-5543-1077. Fax: 03-5543-1078.

NEWLY OPENED — Foreign part-time hall staff needed to work at international-food restaurant. 5:00 p.m.-11:00 p.m. ¥1,200-¥1,400/hour. Japanese-speaking person who can work for 5-6 days/week welcome. Proper visa required. Please apply in person with resume after telephone appointment. Tel: (03) 3406-8410 "Chao! Bamboo" in Roppongi.

DANCERS, HOSTESSES. Tokyo's hottest club, ONE EYED JACKS, is now hiring! Proper Visa Required. Call (03) 5411-2926 after 5:30 p.m.

GAL FRIDAY. Temporary, full time until June, possibly part time thereafter, Native English speaker. (Student visas sharing the job possible). Contact: 3769-3372, noon to 1 p.m. A.I.P.

EXPERIENCED children's teacher required immediately, female, British preferred. Call Hampton School, Shibuya. 03-3406-1252, 10:00 a.m.-7:00 p.m.

Fig. 10. (1 of 2) Sample job advertisements.

Fig. 10. (2 of 2) Sample job advertisements.

been dominated by the big Japanese travel agencies such as JTB and Kintetsu. The influx of foreigners used to buying deeply discounted tickets from 'bucket shops' in London, New York and Hong Kong, combined with the numbers of Japanese discovering how much cheaper airline tickets were overseas, created a demand for the same cheap, no-frills airline ticketing agencies common now in most countries in the West. The result has been the appearance in Japanese cities of small travel agencies offering the cheapest possible prices on airlines and package tours. Since a large percentage of these agencies clientele is foreign, most of them employ a number of foreign staff. Some even employ Japanese speaking foreigners exclusively to run their operations.

Availability   **
Location   Large cities, particularly Tokyo.
Requirements   Experience not often necessary. Japanese language
                      ability is a big plus.
Pay   180,000 + yen monthly, some with benefits.

Waiting/waitressing

Many restaurants in Japan like to enhance their image and appeal by using foreigners as waiters and waitresses. In some hotel restaurants and others popular with resident foreigners and visiting business people and tourists, it is often more effective to use foreign staff who possess both the linguistic and cultural know how to deal with other *gaigin*.

Availability   **
Location   Predominantly Tokyo, Osaka but work also available
                      in Kobe and Yokohama.
Requirements   Pleasant personality and appearance and an ability to
                      deal with people
Pay   1,500-2,000 yen per hour.

7
Working in a Japanese Company

As the employment pattern of foreigners working in Japan changes, many are now finding employment with Japanese companies rather than with subsidiaries or branches of foreign organisations. Joining a Japanese company and working in a wholly Japanese environment comes as a culture shock to most foreigners. Some cope and integrate themselves while others find Japanese working practices too different to their expectations and give notice some time after joining. The Japanese interview process with its series of long meetings and discussion between the employer and prospective employee are designed to give both sides an idea of what to expect from their coming 'betrothal' and also to enable either party to back out if they feel that there is a strong possibility that they will not be compatible with their new 'partner'. Even so, most successful applicants do find much that is different and disorienting inside a Japanese company and this chapter is intended to illuminate some of the things any newcomer to a Japanese organisation should be aware of.

Major differences in approach between a Western and Japanese company

Japanese	Western
Based on groups	Based on individuals
Reward loyalty	Reward success
Stress sincerity	Stress achievement
Tolerate failure	Penalise failure
Bottom up decision-making	Top down decision-making

GENERAL CHARACTERISTICS OF A JAPANESE COMPANY

- Consensus oriented
- Conservative
- Risk averse
- Reward loyalty and long service rather than achievement
- Based on strict hierarchy

Consensus

The organisation of Japanese society is very much based on group decision-making and consensus. It is not too much to say that most Japanese have at least a strong dislike of confrontation and disagreement. It does not follow, however, that Japanese style consensus means that everyone involved in any decision must necessarily agree with that decision. As in most Western companies, final decisions are taken at executive level after (often exhaustive) consultation with lower ranking staff. Japanese style consensus does, however, mean that those who disagree should not continue to express their disagreement once the decision has been reached. Many foreigners working in Japanese companies are pleasantly surprised when they are consulted on some part of company business, particularly when that business may have some connection with their native country. Later, they become disappointed when they find that their recommendations have been apparently ignored. One experienced German, employed by a Japanese pharmaceutical company to aid their export drive into Germany, was consulted at great length over the companies export business plans. 'At the beginning', he says, 'I really felt as if the company was taking note of what I said. I was shocked when the company finally revealed their business plan and just about every point that I had stressed as being important had been ignored. It took me some time to learn that when a Japanese company consults its employees, it is not doing so because it necessarily places great value on their opinions or will act on what its employees say, but because the company wants to be able to be in a position where it can say "You have all been involved in the decision."'

Corporate conservatism

No foreigner should expect to find himself in a Japanese company that has any radical business strategy. Changes that take place within a Japanese organisation, if they take place at all, take place slowly, amongst other reasons to minimise the risk of creating a loss of consensus. Foreigners working in a Japanese business often express their surprise at the fact that while technological advance and innovation in Japan is so rapid, the way

Japanese companies do business seems years behind companies in the West. One foreigner, after joining a Japanese real estate development company, was amazed at the almost total lack of computer literacy among the companies work force. 'While great use was made of the word processing functions of the computers installed at the company, nobody seemed aware that they could generate highly accurate profit and cost analyses if only they would buy in the right spreadsheet software. Instead, profit projections were done laboriously using pencil and paper. Having my own software, I spent some time at home developing a simulation for one project the company was considering and brought it in to the company to show how much quicker and more accurately they could be doing their calculations. My manager told me he was very impressed with my work and how much he wanted to show the company how they could make use of that technology. Eighteen months later, when I left the company, they were still bent over their pencils and paper.'

Risk aversion

Although the 1980s saw the emergence of a number of Japanese businessmen, particularly in the property market willing to make big business gambles (most of which have since failed spectacularly), the vast majority of Japanese businesses remain averse to risk. The very close relationship between Japanese businesses and their bankers is one reason for this, as is the general attitude of Japanese society as a whole toward risk taking. While foreign entrepreneurs who create huge fortunes from taking equally high risks are well known in the Japanese media, they have no Japanese counterparts. Japan's most famous businessmen are all heads of companies that have grown steadily to achieve their current size and prominence over a number of decades, not overnight sensations. An Englishman employed for three years in a Japanese venture capitalist company found that while the company was prepared to receive submissions for higher risk investments, none ever passed through the first stage of considerations. 'Whereas a Western venture capitalist would look at 65-70 per cent success rate as a good track record, the Japanese need to be almost 100 per cent certain they won't lose their money before they make an investment. On the other hand, the returns are nowhere near as good, but this doesn't matter to the Japanese anywhere near as much as does the knowledge that their investment is as secure as it can be.'

Rewards for long service

Although ability and achievement are as much factors in advancement in Japan as elsewhere, they are no guarantee to promotion or pay enhancements in a Japanese company. Salary levels in Japan are based on age and length of service to the company rather than on qualifications or achievement, prior or present. Pay levels for entry level graduates in most Japanese companies are relatively low and only begin to become attractive after the employee has served the company for a number of years, which is one reason why Japanese employees are not tempted to change jobs with the frequency of contemporaries in the West. It is often a source of frustration for foreigners working in Japanese companies that their contribution to the company seems to go unrecognised in terms of pay increases or promotion. As one experienced English equities salesman hired to boost the international savvy of a smaller Japanese securities company put it, 'I worked my end off for two years and made considerably more per capita than any of my Japanese colleagues. But when I pointed this fact out and requested some form of quid pro quo for my efforts, I was told this would create "confusion" among my colleagues, if I were to be treated differently, and that after all, the success was due to the effort of the section as a whole, not just me. The way I look at it, Japanese companies are poor on motivating their employees and maybe even encourage under-achievement. Once you are in, you can get away with doing very little other than going through the motions and still look forward to annual pay increases and promotion. On the other hand, making a significant contribution to the company's bottom line is merely regarded as part of the job and any success is always considered as being achieved by the group not by any one individual.'

'The Japanese take the so-called generation gap seriously', says one American software designer working in a Japanese trading company, or *sho-sha*. 'A 50-year-old Japanese general manager or *bu-cho*, won't take the word of a 27-year-old working in his department. Instead, the 27-year-old will have to communicate through his *shu-nin* who will then pass the word up to his *ka-cho*, who will then tell the *bu-cho*. [See Fig. 11.] Of course, by this time, what the 27-year-old has to say may have gone through a lot of misinterpretation so that what the *bu-cho* finally hears bears little resemblance to the original message. This happened to me a lot. The biggest problem was that I had software design expertise while none of my Japanese superiors did so. While I might be able to get my point through at a face to face, I soon realised that my expertise was being wasted because the people who made the decisions were not getting the right messages.' As the Japanese company bases its system of promotion and rewards on age and years of service, there is very rarely any instance where a superior will find himself wielding authority over an employee older than himself. Many foreigners experience frustration in Japanese

Kai-cho
(Chairman)

Sha-cho
(President)

Komon
(Advisor)

Sodan-yaku
(Advisor)

Fuku-sha-cho
(Vice-President)

Kansa-yaku
(Auditor)

Torishimari-yaku
(Director)

Hon-bu-cho
(Senior General Manager)

Bu-cho
(Department Manager)

Ji-cho
(Assistant Department Manager)

Ka-cho
(Section Manager)

Ka-cho-hosa
(Assistant Section Manager)

Kakari-cho
(Junior Assistant Section Manager)

Shu-nin
(Chief/Group Leader)

Hira
(Untitled rank and file worker)

Fig. 11. Management hierarchy in a Japanese company.

companies due to the fact that they find themselves in a position where they possess greater skill and experience in their assigned role than their Japanese superior but are regarded as subordinates only because of their lack of service to the company in question or simply because of their age.

GENERAL CHARACTERISTICS OF JAPANESE COMPANY WORKERS

- Loyal
- Hard working
- Deferential
- Group centred in approach

Loyalty

Any *sei-sha-in* working for a Japanese company is expected to put his work before every other claim on his time. While the degree of adherence to this unwritten rule differs from individual to individual, it is certainly true that the average Japanese company employee identifies him or herself with his or her company to a far greater extent than an employee working within an American or European business. Japanese employees enter a company with the expectation of remaining in the same organisation for all of their working lives, so it is natural that they tend to see their own personal fortunes and that of their company as being closely related. Many commentators have likened the Japanese company to a family that effectively 'adopts' the new employee as one of its children, with the employees immediate superiors becoming his or her elder brothers and sisters and superiors further up the hierarchy assuming the role of parents, etc. The experience of foreigners on absorption into the system differ, some being positive, others negative. One French woman, employed by a leading Japanese cosmetics company said, 'After hearing how anti-foreign so many Japanese people were, I was happy to find that when I joined the company, everyone did their best to help me sort out whatever problems I had.' Conversely, an American working in a leading Japanese bank remarked that, 'The people I worked with had no conception of life outside the company. Everything they did, even their leisure activities, were done within the umbrella of the bank. Few of them seemed to have any friends outside the bank. I found the whole thing too claustrophobic but the Japanese didn't seem to understand that although I was willing to put a lot of effort into my work, that I needed time away from the company, and away from them too.'

Hard work

Studies have shown that on average, the Japanese put more hours into their work than any of their Western competitors. Behind the veil of hard statistics however, the picture becomes a little more unclear. While there are times when the Japanese work long into the night, for example, prior to company audits and at the end of the financial year, there are many cases when the long hours spent at work do not translate into more work actually being done. As an Englishman working at a Japanese auto maker remarks, 'Many a time the people who worked in the same department as me would not leave until their boss decided to leave, whether there was work to be done or not. It almost seemed as if there was a competition between the section leaders going on, like whose group could stay in the office latest. After six or six thirty though, very little work used to get done. They would smoke, banter with their colleagues, read through the newspapers or trade journals. I used to say, 'Wouldn't you rather be home with your wife and children?' The answer was almost always the same. 'If we went home on time, then our neighbours would begin to gossip. A-san can't be doing well at work because he's coming home early. My wife would hear the gossip and tell me not to come home so early, so I might as well stay here!' As a foreigner and a non-permanent employee, or *shoku-taku*, I found I could live by slightly different rules. Unless I had outstanding work, I would usually go home on time. My colleagues and my boss at work accepted that. I think some of them might even have been a little envious.'

Deference

'The golden rule for survival in a Japanese company,' according to an American with five years of experience in a Japanese utility company, 'is that if you disagree with your department manager, only do it once publicly, then keep your mouth shut unless you want to become very unpopular very quickly. I made the mistake of insisting that my departmental manager was addressing a problem with one of our American suppliers incorrectly. I knew from experience that I was right, but because of the different way the Japanese operate, I didn't know that making plain my opinion in public would cause the manager loss of face. At first I thought I had been caught up in some kind of conspiracy when everyone in the department took the manager's side and told me I was wrong. It was only when my assistant manager took me to one side and told me that everyone knew I was right but we had to think of our manager's seniority and reputation, did I realise that it was my approach that was out of line. The Japanese defer to their superiors and absolutely will not challenge their judgement in front of others. They do it in a more roundabout way, having a quiet word out of earshot, not baldly stating that someone is wrong, but hinting that there might be a better way of doing things. To an American with the bull in a china shop approach to persuasion, the system takes a lot of getting used to. At first I thought it was just time wasting, but having worked here for several years, I now see keeping egos intact is very important in an environment where people have to live with each other for fifteen or twenty years or more.'

Group centredness

The Japanese live by the proverb, 'Find weakness in individuals and strength in groups.' Along with Japanese society itself, Japanese businesses are wholly group oriented. Research, preparation, decision making, execution of business plans are all carried out by groups of workers rather than individuals. An Englishman, hired by a subsidiary of Japan's biggest computer maker, was surprised when shown his desk on his first day in his new job. 'Back in the UK, as a researcher, I had my own office and the degree of privacy that went with it. My desk here was just one of a hundred others in the centre of a big open plan office. The concept of individual endeavour is wholly alien to the Japanese. I remember being very irritated to find one of my work mates going through the contents of the paperwork on my desk, thinking this was an intrusion. The Japanese don't see if that way. You are a member of the team and everyone has access to everybody else's research and materials. I'm sure that this is an advantage in certain cases, but in my field, computer research, I really don't think that the Japanese approach is the most effective.'

THE RIGHT ATTITUDE FOR SUCCESS IN A JAPANESE COMPANY

Flexibility

There is rarely such a thing as a job definition in a Japanese company. Employees are expected to be able to set their hand to whatever is necessary. It is for this reason that the Japanese look for a positive attitude and sincerity in prospective employees (particularly at entry level) rather than proven experience or excellence in one particular field. Most foreigners coming from a Western company background experience a level of resistance when they find they are expected to perform duties which were not a part of the role they were originally hired to perform but this adaptability is seen as normal within a Japanese company and any employee not willing to adapt to a changing role will encounter problems in a Japanese environment.

Tolerance of ambiguity

The root of the ambiguity of Japanese behaviour lies with the Japanese language itself. Japanese language and the cultural rules that govern its use, does not lend itself easily to clear statement of fact. Rather, the language is tied to the situation in which the speaker finds him or herself. An Australian working for an Australian bank's Tokyo branch says, 'When I was first in Japan, I was amazed at how positive and enthusiastic many of the clients I wished to develop were at our first meetings. I was never met with a typical, blunt Australian reply, such as, 'We're not interested.' or 'We already have all the banking services we require.' Instead the Japanese would say things like, 'This is a very interesting proposal.' or 'We'll give this every consideration.' It was only after considerable disappointment when no business materialised that I was told that the Japanese would have considered it rude in the circumstances to turn me down outright. I have since learned that Japanese language is governed by a very different set of social rules to English and one consequence of this is that it is very difficult for a Japanese to say 'No.' Even more frustrating for someone who doesn't understand the rules, the Japanese word for 'yes' can have a number of meanings, such as 'I understand what you're saying, but ...' or merely, 'I see your position.' The bottom line is really to learn as much of the language and the culture that guides it as you can to minimise the chances of making mistakes.'

Tolerance of failure

Most foreigners who work for any time in a Japanese company come to understand that errors and misbehaviour within the company are treated far more leniently than would be the case in a Western or American business. Even continual failure in Japan does not result in dismissal as it would in the West. 'It's all to do with attitude.' pointed out an American working in a Japanese trading company. 'The Japanese will not even consider terminating even the most failure prone employee, as long as there is evidence that the man or woman had acted sincerely. The Japanese solution is to either edge the man or woman in question into a shunting lane where they can do a job of little or no importance and therefore lessen the potential for damage, or to farm him out to a small, subsidiary company whose activities are not crucial to the organisation's core business. It would never happen in the USA, but in Japan, where companies seem to take their social responsibilities more seriously, it is quite commonplace.'

Readiness to work as part of a group

Japanese society is based on groups not individuals, states an English woman working at a Japanese publishing company. 'Everyone here mucks in together and if one member of a team stays late to finish some work, the other members of the team stay late too, even if they have nothing to do. Personally, I think it's great for team spirit. Other foreign people I've met just aren't suited to working as part of a team and that, being uncooperative, is fatal in a Japanese organisation.'

Empathy towards co-workers and business clients

The Japanese language is géared towards seeing the other person's point of view. '*Wakari-mashita*,' reports an English born interpreter, 'is often translated in Japanese English dictionaries as simply, 'I understand'. In fact, in many cases, it means something closer to, 'I understand and appreciate your position however.' It's all a part of the importance of consensus and agreement in Japanese society. Even when the Japanese have to turn someone down, or are in a position where they are turned down, every effort is made to ensure that both sides understand the situation so that one set back doesn't spoil a relationship that may have taken years to build up. In Japan, whether or not you agree or disagree, like or dislike something is neither here nor there, the essential thing is to *understand*.'

Respect

Based to a great extent on Confucian principles, it is not surprising that the Japanese place great stress on respect. One aspect of the Japanese language that many foreigners find difficult to deal with is *kei-go* or 'respect language' that any foreigner must master to be able to claim to speak the language proficiently. Respect permeates all relationships in Japan and within a company, a Japanese worker may use three or four different levels of language within his or her group depending on the age and relative rank of the people with whom he or she is communicating. 'When I was first in Japan,' notes an American lawyer, 'I spoke no Japanese but was always impressed by the level of politeness of the English spoken around me. When I began to take Japanese lessons, I realised that this was a reflection of the important position that respect occupies in the Japanese language. A foreigner who speaks some Japanese can cause great inadvertent offence because of the unsuitable manner in which he chooses to address someone more senior than himself. Fortunately, most Japanese realise how difficult Westerners find that particular aspect of their language and understand that no offence was meant. But I would say that anyone coming from a Western corporate environment who has not had much time for niceties in business needs to invest some time into finding out about the importance of respect to the Japanese before setting foot in the country.'

TYPICAL PROBLEMS OF FOREIGNERS WORKING IN JAPANESE COMPANIES

'I'm not accepted by my fellow workers'

Most foreigners themselves regard a job in Japan with a Japanese company as a stepping stone to something better rather than a job for life. The relatively high turnover of foreign *shoku-taku* in Japanese companies (the average foreign worker stays for 18 months to 3 years) leaves many Japanese with the impression that there is little value in investing time and effort into developing a working relationship with a *gaigin* because they will soon move on to their next job. Some foreigners have noted that after serving their first year at a company, the attitude of their Japanese co-workers toward them began to change for the better. Others have found that as their grasp of the language improved and they were able to communicate to their colleagues in Japanese, relations improved considerably.

'I get no thanks for a job well done'

The Japanese do not conceive of success in terms of individuals but in terms of groups, so unlike the West, no Japanese boss will single out one member of the group as the person responsible for achievement. One American woman noted that this habit also has a plus side. Having made a serious error in an order from abroad for one of her trading company's clients, she was not held personally responsible. The group was held responsible for the failure and everyone accepted that she alone did not bear any special responsibility. In an American company, she felt, she could well have faced dismissal.

'I don't stand a chance of promotion'

Most foreigners joining a Japanese company will do so as *shoku-taku*, which automatically disbars them from any opportunity of promotion. Even among those who join as a *sei-sha-in*, the chances of rising up the executive ladder are comparatively slim, again because Japanese expectations are that a foreign worker has no intention of devoting more than a few years at most to the company. One English *sei-sha-in*, having worked in a Japanese real estate company for two years was promoted to a management position because, as he says, he had proved that he was committed to the company, spoke the language fluently and most importantly, had shown everyone at the company that he was as good, if not better, at his work in the company's international department as any of his Japanese co-workers.

8
Getting Established in Japan

Finding a job in Japan is only the first of several steps you must take before you can consider yourself established. Once you are working, you will also have to spend time and money getting the rest of your life organised. Your first requirement will be to find somewhere to live on a more permanent basis.

FINDING ACCOMMODATION

Unless you have access to extra funds to enable you to move straight into permanent accommodation, you will probably have to spend an extra month living in your temporary accommodation waiting to replenish your funds from your first salary. Alternatively, if your employer is prepared to offer you a loan, taking advantage of this would allow you to get settled in more quickly. Setting up your accommodation will probably be your biggest expense in Japan so you should make absolutely sure that you find exactly what you want before making a decision.

Taking your pick: Japanese or Western?

Most Japanese dwellings area an amalgamation of Japanese, or *wa-fu*, and Western, or *yo-fu*, styles and some detached houses and bigger apartments will have a 'Japanese' room, floored with traditional *tatami* matting set aside for special occasions and another, Western style room, carpeted and fitted out with sofas, chairs and electronics for everyday living. Accommodation providing Western features has grown dramatically in the last ten years. In the case of smaller accommodation, the choices between Japanese and Western are as follows:

Living/bedrooms: Japanese rooms will feature *tatami* matted floorings,
traditional *oshi-ire* built in cupboards with sliding paper
doors. Entry into the rooms will also be through
Japanese style *fusuma*, sliding doors.. Japanese rooms
tend to be easy on the eye and also, given the extremely
humid Japanese summers, provide some relief from the

heat. On the other hand, winter in a Japanese style home can be very cold. Western style rooms will be carpeted. Cupboards will have doors and entry will usually be via a plastic concertina door. As the carpet is usually laid directly onto a concrete base, it does not provide much in the way of comfort. *Tatami*, which is made to be sat on, is much softer.

Toilets: Traditional Japanese toilets are of the 'squat' variety. Although physiologically more healthy than the Western pedestal toilet, some foreigners prefer to use the latter.

Bathrooms: Japanese baths fall into two categories, reheatable and non-reheatable. The Japanese wash and rinse themselves before entering the bath which means that the same water can be used a number of times if it can be re-heated. A bath featuring a gas circulator to boost the water temperature can be a big saver.

What is available?

There are basically three types of accommodation available:

- detached houses, or *iken-ya*
- concrete-built apartment blocks or *mansion*
- wood-constructed apartment blocks, or *apaa-to.*

Detached houses

Although concrete is being used more and more as a building material for family homes, the vast majority of Japanese detached houses are still built around a wooden frame. As in most major cities around the world, the price of land limits all but the most expensive detached homes to the suburbs and even there, renting is still expensive. Those *iken-ya* which are centrally located are expensive enough to be unfeasible unless you are coming to Japan on a generous expatriate package. Some 'bargain' detached houses are available on the rentals market for short lets of one to two years. These are usually buildings that are 30 to 35 years old and therefore, (in Japanese terms) considered too old for habitation. Most of these dwellings turn out to be 'livable' if inconvenient compared to modern housing. All will be Japanese in style. Such buildings do exist in city centres, but they are extremely rare and more usually found away from the city.

Pros

- Normally more spacious than other forms of accommodation.
- Comparably more privacy.

Cons

- Expensive.
- Unlikely to be available in central locations.

Mansion

The Japanese have borrowed the term '*mansion*' to describe concrete constructed apartment blocks. Sizes of the accommodation offered varies from studios, or 'one room *mansions*' up to big units with five or six rooms. The blocks themselves also vary from small, three or four storey buildings up to the largest *mansion* with fifteen floors or more. The biggest of all, built in the 1960s and early 1970s and housing several hundred separate dwellings are known as *danchi*. As in the West, this form of housing is no longer popular and the trend is towards lower density constructions. Japanese construction regulations dictate that any *mansion* with more than five floors must provide one or more lifts for the residents.

Pros

- Cheaper relative to *iken-ya*.
- Centrally located *mansions* available.

Cons

- Less privacy.
- Less space.

Apaa-to

If the word '*apaa-to*' sounds vaguely familiar, it is because it is borrowed from the English word, apartment. The Japanese use the term to describe a particular kind of accommodation; a small, wood constructed, two storey block of small units, normally with no more than two or three rooms each. Most *apaa-to* available for rent will be Japanese in style although a fair proportion of those built within the last five years will offer western features. *Apaa-to* are the most widespread form of rented accommodation in Japan and can be found almost everywhere.

Pros

- Available in all locations.
- Cheapest form of accommodation.

Cons

- Least privacy.
- Cold in winter.

Establishing your priorities

Before you begin to look for accommodation, you should have a clear idea of what kind of place you want, where you want it and how much you are willing to pay for it. The points you should consider are listed below:

- How much rent can you afford?
- How far are you willing to travel to and from work?
- How far are you willing to live from the railway or underground station line you will use to commute?
- Is distance from shopping facilities important to you?
- How much space do you need?
- Do you have a preference for Western style accommodation over Japanese?
- What sort of neighbourhood do you want to live in?
- Are you prepared to forego air conditioning?

Calculating what you can afford

The monthly cost of accommodation in Japan as a proportion of income generally works out at around 20-30 per cent. Therefore, if you are receiving a salary of 350,000 yen, you should plan to spend no more than 70,000-100,000 yen on your accommodation. If your employer is willing to subsidise part of the cost, you may be able to afford something more expensive.

Zoning your accommodation

Once you have decided how much time you are prepared to spend commuting to and from work, you will be in a position to determine which areas are within travelling distance of your company. Taking station to station time in a major city such as Tokyo and Osaka as approximately four minutes, you will be able to calculate how far away from your company you will be able to live. Using a city map, you will then be able to find out which areas along which railway or subway lines, best suits your needs.

Once you have found answers to these questions, you will be in a better position to decide where to begin your search.

Getting to and from your local station

The price of a *mansion* or *apaa-to* can vary quite substantially depending on the distance from the local station. You can expect to pay a premium rent for anything within ten minutes walking distance of the station. Conversely, the rental for accommodation located a fifteen-minute bus ride from the station will be correspondingly lower due to the inconvenience. You may be tempted to go for the cheaper option, but bear in mind that a bus ride will add to your travel time and be inconvenient when you are in a hurry.

Meeting your everyday needs

Japan boasts more retail outlets than any other country and wherever you live, you will find one of the ubiquitous 'convenience' stores, or a 'mom and pop' corner shop, nearby. Bear in mind however that these small stores are more expensive than shopping at one of Japan's several chains of supermarkets and that variety will always be limited. Bigger stores are almost always located near to a station.

Thinking about space

Most people have heard about the cramped living conditions of the Japanese and to an extent, it is true that accommodation is rarely generously sized, and when it is, it comes with a premium price attached. However, most Tokyo *apaa-to* compare favourably in size (and price) to a studio or one bedroom flats found in London, Paris or New York. Generally speaking, most foreigners adapt very quickly to Japanese sized living spaces. In Japan, people tend to spend far less time at home than compared to Western countries as most socialising is also done outside the home. Bearing this in mind, you should think carefully before committing yourself to paying a higher rent for a few extra square metres of space.

Japanese or Western?

Recent trends indicate that Western style accommodation is becoming more popular, particularly among the younger Japanese. In some respects, Western style accommodation is more convenient and less prone to wear and tear. On the other hand, some people say that carpeted *apaa-to* and mansion get much more humid in summer than those laid with *tatami*. If you opt for *tatami*, then you will also be opting for a Japanese *futon* mattress for sleeping rather than the bed and mattress arrangement you are probably used to. *Futon* are usually sold in two parts. The *shiki-buton* forms the upper part and is usually well stuffed with cotton, or polyester in the cheaper version. These are currently popular in the UK and other Western countries. However, many people find them uncomfortable, saying that they are too hard. This is because the *shiki-buton* is not meant to be sold alone but in tandem with a mattress, or *mato-resu*, as the Japanese pronounce it. The *mato-resu* is a thin, foam-filled version of a Western style mattress, normally sewn into four sections so that it can be folded away during the daylight hours along with the *shiki-buton*, in the *apaa-to's* store cupboard, or *oshi-ire*. The *shiki-buton*, on top of a *mato-resu* and with soft *tatami* underneath make for a very comfortable sleeping arrangement and even the most sceptical of newcomers usually end up singing the combination's praises. Alternatively, if you choose to rent a mansion, you will probably find it has a concrete floor covered only with a thin laying of laminated wooden flooring or an equally thin carpet. In this case, due to the hardness of the floor, a bed might begin to make more sense.

Choosing your neighbourhood
When you have established how close to your place of work you can afford to live, you should begin to think about the area in which you wish to be based. Like cities all over the world, the character of Tokyo and Osaka change from area to area. The western suburbs of Tokyo, for example, tend to be newer and more cosmopolitan than the more traditional, conservative areas in the east districts. Ask around, and most importantly, use the transport system to take a good look at each area within your travelling zone to get a good idea of which locations most appeal to you.

Air conditioning
The hot and very humid Japanese summer makes air conditioning a very desirable mod con in a Japanese *apaa-to* or mansion. Air conditioners come in two types, *rei-bo* and *rei-dan-bo*. The former functions only as an air cooler, while the latter combines this function with a heating facility that is useful in the winter. Air conditioning does push up the price of accommodation, usually by 5,000-10,000 yen per month, not including the electricity expended to run it. Some people aver that a summer in Japan would be unbearable without the prospect of a cool room to return to at night, others warn that the chill of an air conditioned room in the summer evenings is a sure fire way to catch a nasty cold.

Where to look for your accommodation

In Japan, rented accommodation is offered almost exclusively through real estate agencies, or *fudo-san-ya*. Most *fudo-san-ya* orient their services towards Japanese although there are a number of agencies, all in urban areas, that offer a service for foreign residents. There are some chains of *fudo-san-ya*, but the majority are small, one-man operations. Offices are usually located conspicuously around the exits from railway and subway stations.

DECODING THE LANGUAGE OF JAPANESE PROPERTY

Flyers advertising Japanese property can be found displayed in the windows of every *fudo-san-ya* as well as being pasted on telegraph poles and hoardings. All these advertisements follow a set format which is comprehensible given a few minutes preparation.

Japanese property is described in terms of size and the number of rooms available.

Size: The size of accommodation is measured in terms of *jo* and *tsubo*. A *jo* is equal in size to one Japanese *tatami* mat, measuring roughly six feet by three. A *tsubo* is equal to two *jo*. Most rooms are of a standard size, being either four and a half, six, eight or ten *jo*, with six being the norm.

Rooms: K   = Kitchen
             DK = Dining/Kitchen
             LDK = Living room and Dining/Kitchen.

For example, a mansion advertised as 2LDK would comprise a living room, dining/kitchen plus two other rooms.

How the prices are determined

The level of rent set for any house, mansion or *apaa-to* depends on much the same set of factors:

● distance from the city or town centre
● size of the property
● features/equipment included
● age of structure
● distance from the station
● distance from amenities.

Taking these factors into account, you may find that unless you are prepared to accept a very small or old *apaa-to* with few facilities, you will not be able to live as close to your workplace as you would like. Most people in Japan, Japanese and foreign alike, usually find themselves obliged to live at least an hour's travelling time from their work due to the cost of centrally located property.

Considering the costs

While the actual monthly rental for Japanese accommodation may seem fairly reasonable compared with what you are used to, the up front costs of renting accommodation in Japan are likely to be far higher that you have experienced in your own country. These costs are known by the foreign community in Japan as 'key money', meaning the costs that have to be incurred before the owner of the property seals a rental contract with you and hands over the keys to the accommodation. Japanese property is by and large a sellers market and that fact is reflected in the way that payments are structured.

Cost breakdown

'Thank you' money, or rei-kin

Rei-kin is a once only charge, equal to one month's rent, payable by the renter to the landlord. As the translation implies, the payment is meant to express your gratitude to the owner for allowing you to rent his or her property. *Rei-kin* is non-refundable.

Deposit or shiki-kin

Shiki-kin is a refundable deposit paid to the owner by the renter and serves two purposes. First, any damage caused by the renter during occupation will be made good by using part of the *shiki-kin*. Second, if the renter vacates the accommodation without giving the appropriate notice as included in the rental contract (normally one month, sometimes longer) then a part, or all, the *shiki-kin* will be held back to cover the owner's loss of rental. The amount of *shiki-kin* demanded is usually equal to two month's rent although occasionally, only one month's is considered sufficient.

Agent's commission, or teh-su-ryo

In Japan, it is the renter, not the owner, who pays the estate agent who brought the two sides together. *Teh-su-ryo* is equal to one month's rental.

Rental in advance

Along with the above costs, the renter is also obliged to pay one month's rental in advance.

Taking the example of a 2DK *apaa-to* situated in Kichijoji, a suburb of western Tokyo popular with the foreign community with a monthly rental of 75,000 yen, the amount up front costs payable prior to closing the rental contract will be:

Rei-kin:	75,000 yen (non-refundable)
Shiki-kin:	150,000 yen (refundable)
Teh-su-ryo:	75,000 yen (non-refundable)
Rent in advance:	75,000 yen
Total:	375,000 yen

The Japanese have an expression, *hikkoshi bimbo*, meaning to become poor through changing address too often.   Considering the costs associated with finding accommodation, you will appreciate how important it is that you take the time to find a place that is exactly what you require. As you can see, mistakes come expensive!

VISITING AN ESTATE AGENT

Even if you speak fairly good Japanese, it is a good idea to ask along a native speaker. If you are destined to meet with discrimination against foreigners in Japan, the chances are that you will encounter it at the *fudo-san-ya*. Taking along a Japanese national to assure the estate agent of your reliability should minimise the risk of your home hunting turning into a nasty experience. Even so, you may be told as soon as you enter that none of the *fudo-san-ya's* clients are willing to deal with foreigners. Whether or not this is true, there is nothing you can do about it except to turn around, walk out of the door and down the street to the next agent. A considerable number of *fudo-san-ya* specialising in letting to foreigners exist in the big city centres, particularly Tokyo and a short list of the leading operations is included in the Appendix. You should note however that these agents usually offer accommodation that is somewhat more expensive than what you can expect to find on the books of a Japanese *fudo-san-ya*.

The *fudo-san-ya* lays out his wares in his window. Before going inside, examine all the rentals on offer. If any take your eye, then go inside and ask, or get your Japanese companion to ask when it would be convenient to view. It is not usually necessary to make an appointment. The agent will accompany you, either by car or on foot to the property for you to see if it is what you require. It is always preferable to view accommodation during daylight hours rather than in the evening.

What to look for
Another benefit of being accompanied by a Japanese is that you have a pair of experienced eyes alongside you able to judge whether the accommodation on offer will meet your needs and, just as important, whether it represents value for money. Listed below are some key points to check as you look over your prospective home.

- If you walk from the estate agency to the property, time how long it takes. The walking times listed on rental advertisements are often inaccurate. If you go by car, ask the agent the location of the nearest bus stop and check on the frequency of buses to the station.

- Take a look at the area around the property for late night 'snack' or *karaoke* bars. In Japan, such establishments often stay open until the early hours causing inconvenience for those living nearby.

- Check the attitude of the property. Most Japanese prefer south facing, or *minami muke*, windows as these mean more natural light during the daytime.

- In the kitchen, check for appliances and furniture, if any, being offered with the accommodation. If a gas hobs and/or kitchen cupboards or shelving are provided, this will save you some expense. Washing machines are usually sited on a balcony or entry walkway. Check to see if one is supplied.

- In the bathroom, check whether the *o-furo* is of the reheatable type or not.

- In the living/bedrooms, check the condition of the carpeting and/or *tatami* for signs of wear. Similarly check any fixtures and fittings.

- Check whether or not a combined air heater/conditioner is connected into the accommodations main room/s. In summer, due to the high heat and humidity, an air conditioner is highly desirable.

- Check whether rigid insect nets are attached to all windows and that none of them are holed. You will need to keep windows open in the heat of the summer, but due to the large number of mosquitoes, nets are essential.

Closing the deal

Once you have decided on the place you like and the agent has got the agreement of the owner, things take place fairly quickly. Rentals contracts are standard agreements covering no more than five sides of A4. It is nevertheless vital that you get someone to read over the contract and describe to you the terms and conditions being offered. You should particularly pay close attention to the following points.

- The monthly rent. The amount and how and when it is payable.

- Maintenance payments. Are you obliged to pay anything extra for the up-keep of the building in which your *mansion* or *apaa-to* is contained?

- Period of notice. How much warning you need to give your landlord of your intention to move out. Remember that failure to give the requisite notice could result in the loss of a part, or all, of your two month's deposit. Also, check whether or not the contract states whether notice will be accepted verbally or if it must be given in writing.

- Conditions of renewal. What, if any, extra monies are payable if you renew your rental contract after the expiry of the initial two year period.

- Items listed on the inventory of appliances, furniture if supplied with the accommodation. You should check to ensure that the items are actually available and that they are in good working order.

You will find a typical advertisement for a Japanese *mansion* in Fig. 12. Almost all advertisements follow the same basic format, so use this as a key when you start looking for your accommodation. Looking at the floor plan of the *mansion*, you will see that it is a 2DK, i.e. a dining kitchen, one 6 *jo* room and one 4.5 *jo* room. The *mansion* is in Motoyawata, a suburb of Tokyo just over the border of Chiba-ken, east of the city and a popular area. The rent of 75,000 yen monthly is quite high, but note that the *mansion* is within walking distance of a main line station with direct access to central Tokyo, which is considered a big plus. The 'thank you' money and the deposit are standard at two months rent each. The accommodation features most conveniences but note that it lacks air conditioning.

Looking at other options

Nobody likes to have to spend the equivalent of two months hard earned salary to get a roof over their head. Alternatives to the *fudo-san-ya* route do exist in Japan, but the chances are that you will find yourself having to *gaman suru* and pay out your *rei-kin, shiki-kin* and *teh-su-ryo* anyway.

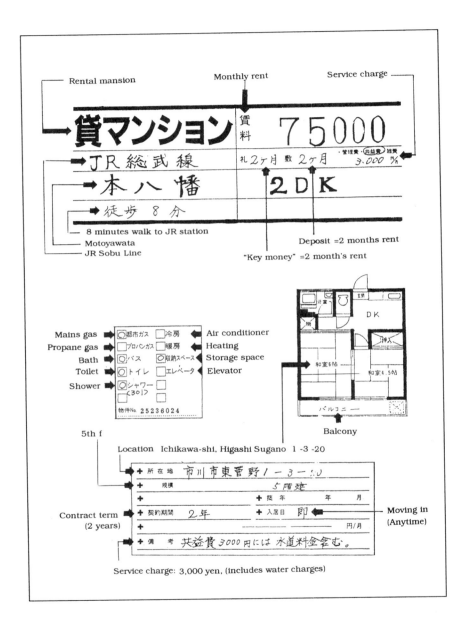

Fig. 12. Sample advertisement of accommodation.

Short stay accommodation

Several years ago, some of the estate agents specialising in letting to *gaigin* begin to realise that many foreigners were reluctant to pay 'key money' for a two year rental contract when they expected to be staying in Japan only a year or less. In conjunction with some landlords and property developers, these agents began to offer short stay *mansions*, mainly aimed at visiting *gaigin*. These *mansions* are normally centrally located studios or one bedroom properties. Most of them are modern and better equipped than a *mansion* or *apaa-to* offered by a typical Japanese *fudo-san-ya*. The great advantage of the short stay *mansion* is that the renter is not obliged to pay any up front monies either to the landlord or to the estate agent. The downside of this arrangement is that the monthly rental is correspondingly higher, sometimes up to 30 per cent more than you could expect to pay for a comparable property contracted according to the usual Japanese way. This higher rent compensates the landlord and agent for the loss of *rei-kin* and *teh-su-ryo* respectively and also reflects the extra equipment provided with the accommodation. Depending on the agent and the property involved, refundable *shiki-kin*, usually equal to two weeks or one month's rent is payable prior to an agreement being reached.

Pros

- No 'key money' payments to landlord.
- Usually, no *teh-su-ryo* payment to the agent.
- Better level of equipment than usual.

Cons

- Considerably higher monthly rent.

The way to calculate whether a short stay *mansion* is for you, is to make an estimation of how long you intend to stay in Japan and then compare what you would pay over that period renting in the normal way and renting a short stay apartment.

For example, imagine that you had found a job in the Shinjuku district of Tokyo and that the initial term of contract is for one year. You do not wish to spend more than thirty minutes travelling each way to work so you settle on the Nakano district west of Shinjuku as your target area for accommodation. Central Nakano is too expensive, but as you are only fifteen minutes away from your company in Shinjuku, you decide to live at a distance from Nakano station and travel in daily by bus. You find a recently completed 2K apartment that you like. The monthly rent is 80,000 yen, so you would be facing the following payments before you are able to seal a two year rental contract.

Rei-kin:	80,000 yen	(equivalent to one month's rent, non-refundable)
Shiki-kin:	160,000 yen	(equivalent to two months' rent, refundable)
Teh-su-ryo:	80,000 yen	(equivalent to one month's rent, non-refundable)
Rent:	80,000 yen	
Total:	400,000 yen	

As you are not happy with the idea of paying out so much money, you look round for an alternative and find a short stay 2K *mansion* in the same area. The monthly rental is 100,000. No up front money is required except for a refundable *shiki-kin* equal to two weeks' rent and one month's rent in advance.

Shiki-kin:	50,000 yen	(equivalent to two weeks' rent, refundable)
Rent:	100,000 yen	
Total:	150,000 yen.	

Clearly, the short stay *mansion* seems like a more attractive proposition. But when you calculate what you would be paying over the year, you realise that in fact, the apartment that you found first ends up as the cheaper option despite the up front costs incurred. On the other hand, if you intend to stay for eight months or less, it is the short stay apartment that is more economical.

Unless you really intend to stay no longer than six months or so in Japan, the short stay *mansion* system is probably not for you. It is the experience of most *gaigin* who have come to Japan and stayed in such accommodation, that they invariably end up staying much longer than they had first anticipated and end up paying over the odds for their accommodation as a result.

The Japan Housing Corporation

The Japan Housing Corporation builds, rents out and manages what would be termed as council accommodation in the UK. The rents on these *mansion* and *apaa-to* are subsidised that therefore considerably cheaper than what is available privately. Many of the Housing Corporation's properties are located very close to city centres and as such they are in great demand. The only way to secure accommodation through this scheme is to buy a ticket and enter one of the four lotteries run in February, May, August and November to select the lucky winners. Once ensconced in this low cost accommodation, people tend to stay put so the chance of being lucky enough to pick a winning ticket are correspondingly low, 12,600 to 1 according to one Japanese daily.

Company dormitory

Many larger Japanese companies offer their employees subsidised dormitory, or *shataku*, accommodation. *Shataku* for single employees is invariably in single sex apartment blocks, and usually no more than 1DK in size. 2DK and larger accommodation is reserved for employees with families.

Pros

- Usually close to workplace.
- Cheaper than privately rented accommodation of comparable size.
- Often furnished with basic necessities.

Cons

- Can become claustrophobic.
- Accommodation often inferior to that available privately.

MOVING IN THE JAPANESE WAY

Once all the required payments have been made and both sides have put their name stamps to, or signed the contract, you will receive a set of keys to your accommodation. When you move to your new home, it would be a good idea to do things the Japanese way and introduce yourself to your new neighbours. Japanese etiquette dictates that the new arrival present his or her neighbours with a small gift. Department stores carry ready wrapped 'stock gifts' of small hand towels at around 500 yen each. Being a foreigner, you are not expected to conform to his custom although your neighbours would probably be pleasantly surprised if you did!

FURNISHING YOUR HOME

Once you have moved into your new *mansion* or *apaa-to*, you will be faced with the need to provide yourself with the basic necessities and one or two luxuries as well.

Essentials	**Luxuries**
Two burner gas hob*	Television*
Fridge*	Electronic rice cooker*
Heater*	Video recorder*
Futon or bed	Table lamp*
Kitchen table and chairs*	*Kotatsu*, heated table*
China	
Pots and pans	
Cabinets/shelving*	
Telephone*	
Electric fan*	

As you will have only just spent a considerable amount of money getting your accommodation, it is fortunate that alternatives exist to going to the local department store and spending another small fortune buying in what you need. All the above items marked with an asterisk are available from other sources, either at much cheaper prices, or best of all, for free. The only items not marked with an asterisk are futon/bed, china and pots and pans which are always best bought new. Try the big supermarkets like Daiei or Seiyu where you should be able to pick up these goods quite cheaply. Although you may not feel keen on buying used goods, bear in mind that you may stay in Japan no longer than one or two years and that objects purchased new will hold no more that 20 per cent at the most of their original price if sold as secondhand goods.

Getting things for free

As in any consumer society, the Japanese often find themselves with appliances and furniture that they no longer consider desirable. However, due to the size of most homes and the fact that attic and garage space is hardly ever utilised for storage, there is very rarely any other option than to throw out objects no longer considered to be of use. As a consequence, many appliances and items of furniture discarded by Japanese households still have years of use ahead of them. This is where you come in.

Refuse collection in Japan is rather more complicated than what you are used to. In order to promote more recycling and cut down on the amount of waste poured into landfill sites on their crowded islands, the Japanese have divided up refuse into four categories.

Burnable refuse, or moeru gomi

Moeru gomi basically means vegetable matter and paper packaging.

Non-burnable refuse, or moenai gomi

Moenai gomi includes plastics and metals of all kinds and any other non-organic materials.

When you move into your new home, one of the first things you must do is find out on which days *moeru gomi* and *moenai gomi* are collected. In Japan, rules exist to be obeyed and although you will not be breaking any laws, you will be unpopular both with the refuse collectors and with your neighbours if you ignore the rules and simply bundle everything up together, or put out *moenai gomi* on the day when *moeru gomi* is collected.

Newspapers, magazines and clothing

Newspapers, magazines and clothing are set aside and put out separate to other refuse. Check your neighbourhood for details.

Large refuse, or sodai gomi

Large items of refuse are put out for collection once every month. You will regularly find the items marked with asterisks put out on *sodai gomi* day, almost all of them in good working order. To take advantage of this unintentional largess, find out when the *sodai gomi* is collected in your area and the collection point. Most *sodai gomi* is put out on the day before collection. If you make a visit to the collection point late in the evening, you should find several things that you could make good use of. The most important point is not to be shy. There is no negative connation attached to recycling other people's furniture and appliances in Japan, so if you find something you need and can make good use of, take it.

Recycle and secondhand stores

Although not available free, you will also be able to find a lot of used items of furniture and electrical appliances in recycle stores or secondhand shops, or *chuko-ya*. These outlets are especially common in areas where students live.

Furniture stores

When the Japanese renew some item of furniture, the piece they are replacing is usually collected by the store from which the new item was purchased. A look around the back of a big furniture retailer normally reveals a number of such items awaiting collection. As the retailer often has to pay for these items to be removed, he or she is normally happy to give them to you gratis or for a nominal sum.

The Salvation Army

If you find yourself living in Tokyo, then you may find many of the items you require at the Salvation Army's large recycling warehouse near Nakano in western Tokyo. The address and telephone number of the warehouse are in the Appendix.

A note about televisions

A large proportion of the programmes televised in Japan are imported, principally from America, but also from other sources, notably the BBC. One of the not to be under-estimated benefits of living in Japan is that many of these imports are broadcast simultaneously with both the script or narrative in its original version as well as with the Japanese voiceover. In order for you to receive the programme in its original language, you will need a television with a bilingual or *nikka-koku-go* facility. Originally, these sets were prohibitively expensive but now many of the TV sets on sale have *nikka-koku-go* as standard. If you are considering buying a new or used set, it is well worth getting one with this facility.

Getting a telephone installed

After spending so much money on accommodation, another shock is in store for the new to Japan *gaigin*. In order to have a telephone line installed, it is necessary to pay the Nippon Telephone Company, or NTT as everyone knows it, 80,000 yen. This sum buys you ownership of a telephone line, although a further payment is necessary, around another 20,000 yen, to actually get the line installed. Due to the expense involved, it is certainly worth asking whether your employer would be willing to purchase the line on your behalf.

Buying 'used' lines

NTT is always willing to sell lines but will not buy them back. This gap has been filled by small line broking companies who buy lines at a discount from those who no longer require them and then sell them on to a third party at a price that is discounted compared to the price of a new line direct from NTT.

Alternatively, it is often possible to find another *gaigin* who is preparing to leave Japan and has a line to sell. You can always do a deal over a telephone line with an individual which costs you less and leaves the seller with more than if you had gone through a broker.

TYING UP LOOSE ENDS

If you have moved into a different *-ku* or *-shi* from where you were staying previously, you must remember to go to the *kuyaku-sho* or *shiyaku-sho* that administers the area where you are now residing, so that the details of your *gaigin touroku-sho* can be changed and your new address registered.

Do not be surprised if you receive a visit from the local policeman, or *o-mawari-san*, some time after you have moved in. Great stress is placed on community policing in Japan and most new residents receive a visit, so that the police can get acquainted with the new arrivals. If the police do pay you a visit, inviting them in for a cup of tea or coffee is considered proper etiquette.

BUYING AND USING A CAR IN JAPAN

The first thing to be said about owning and running a car in Japan is that if you find yourself living in Tokyo, Osaka or any of Japan's larger cities, you will probably have very little need of a car as the excellent public transport system will more than meet your needs for transportation. But for those who live in less urbanised areas of Japan and those who don't but want a car nevertheless, it is worth first considering the responsibilities that come with car ownership in Japan.

Licences
There are two licences which a foreign resident can use in Japan.

International Driver's Licence
International driver's licence must be purchased in your country of origin. In the UK, they are available from branches of the Automobile Association. You will need to produce a valid UK driving licence and a photograph. The charge for the issue of the licence is at present £3 and the licence is valid for one year from the date of issue.

Japanese Driver's Licence
As an international licence only lasts for one year, if you are planning to stay longer than that in Japan, it is probably best to apply for a Japanese driver's licence once you have arrived in Japan. The only condition necessary for an application to be accepted is that you have had a driver's

licence from your country of origin for more than three months. Japanese driver's licence are issued by the regional and metropolitan motor vehicle section of the police force. You will need to show your current driver's licence. A Japanese driver's licence is valid for five years from the date of issue. A sample licence is shown in Fig. 13.

Parking spaces

Due to lack of space in most Japanese cities and the chronic traffic congestion that they suffer, most areas now insist on car buyers either buying or renting off road parking space before they purchase a car. This means that if you do not provide yourself with a parking space and documentation to prove you have one, no car dealer will be able to sell you a car, used or new. Parking spaces are not cheap. It is now quite usual for Japanese landlords to offer parking spaces as an optional extra together with the *mansion* or *apaa-to* they are offering for rent. In central Tokyo, parking space monthly rental of 15,000 yen and above (£100+) is not unusual.

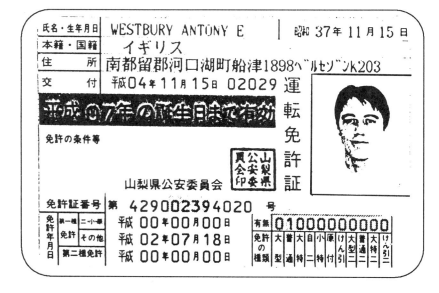

Fig.13. Sample Japanese driving licence.

Car tax

Car tax in Japan is payable annually every April. The amount paid differs according to the model and size of the vehicle being taxed. Car tax on an average 2 litre saloon would cost approximately 40,000 yen (£250). Unlike the UK however, car tax is regarded as the possession of the car owner. Accordingly, when a car is sold in Japan, it is sold untaxed, the owner retaining the tax for his next vehicle.

Sha-ken

Sha-ken is the Japanese equivalent of the UK MOT vehicle inspection system. Any car reaching its third year of registration must be put through the *sha-ken* inspection and once every two years thereafter. *Sha-ken* is expensive, costing 120,000 yen (£700) for an average family saloon. This cost varies according to how much work the inspectors deem necessary for the vehicle to be passed as fit for use.

Japanese car insurance

Approximately half of the cost of *sha-ken* comprises the compulsory purchase of two years of insurance, known as *jibai-zaki*, meaning that if a car has passed it *sha-ken* inspection, it will automatically be insured and can be legally driven. However, as *jibai-zaki* insurance is limited to first party accident and damage and the amounts payable are limited, most Japanese drivers take out secondary insurance, known as *ni-in hoken* with private insurers, which provides broader cover and higher payment ceilings. Typical *ni-in hoken* on an average family saloon would cost around 60,000 yen (£350) per year depending on age and vehicle type. No claims bonuses of 10 per cent can also reduce the overall cost of insurance.

9
Looking after your Financial Affairs

ARRANGING JAPANESE BANKING SERVICES

The names of the major Japanese banks are nowadays known throughout the world. Within Japan, a second tier of smaller banks exist, making a wide choice available to Japanese consumers. The services these banks offer are much the same as banks operating in any Western economy with one significant exception.

The Japanese banking system and personal cheques

Despite the growing popularity of credit cards, Japan is still very much a cash society, due perhaps to the relative lack of street crime. Unlike countries such as the UK, the concept of personal cheques has never developed in Japan, where cheques are only issued for large amounts (millions of yen) by companies. When you open up an account with a Japanese bank, do not therefore be surprised when you are not offered a cheque book and card.

Because of the rarity of personal cheques passing through the banking system, especially foreign cheques, it is also time consuming and costly (due to the bank's charges) to transfer money from home in cheque form. Both telegraphic transfer and traveller's cheques are faster and cost less in terms of commission.

Starting an account

Although there are branches of foreign banks in Japan, they do not exist to carry out retail banking services to individuals. Therefore, it will be most convenient, both for you and for your employer if you set up an account with a Japanese bank. Setting up an account with a Japanese bank is no different to doing so at home. To open an account you will need to take the following to present to the bank:

- proof of identity (passport or *gaigin* card)
- first deposit (1,000 yen is sufficient).

What you get

Once the formalities have been completed, the bank will present you with a bank book with your first deposit entered. You will also receive a cash card through the post for use in the bank's cashing machines along with those of most other banking institutions. One advantage of the Japanese system is that at the time of opening your account, you are asked to select your own Personal Identity Number, meaning that you choose a number which is easiest for you to remember. Your paying in book can be used inside the bank, or alternatively at the cash dispensers, to deposit money or to get an update of your banking transactions.

Because Japanese banks are in a highly competitive market and take the idea of customer service seriously, you will probably also receive a thank you gift for opening an account, normally an assortment of paper tissues, note books, pens and pencils.

Doing it the Japanese way

The Japanese rarely put their signature to any document. Instead, they identify themselves by the use of a name stamp, or *hanko*. Most Japanese surnames consist of two Chinese characters, or *kanji*. These are formed onto the bottom of the *hanko* and printed onto documents by the use of a red ink pad, or *shuniku*. This name stamp is then used in much the same way as a Westerner would put his signature to any document. As the Japanese system is designed to accept name stamps rather than signatures, you could make life a lot simpler for yourself (not to mention less confusing for Japanese bank clerks!) if you had your own name stamp made up. The *hanko* can be made of stone, wood or, cheapest of all, plastic. The use of ivory for *hanko*, once commonplace, is now banned. The best place to find cheap plastic *hanko* is in the local stationers, or *bunbo-guya*. Here you will find hundreds of ready made plastic *hanko* covering the most Japanese family names. Many *bunbo-guya* will also make up a *hanko* to your order for around £10-15.

Choosing a name

Most Western names can be broken down into their constituent syllables and then reformed using Chinese *kanji* characters. For example, the author's name, Hayter, was broken down into Hei- and Ta- and then made up again into the Japanese version using two *kanji* with the same pronunciations.

Applying for a credit card

Despite the traditional Japanese preference for cash, credit cards such as Visa, Mastercard and American Express have all made inroads into Japan, particularly among the younger generation. Many banks now give new account holders the option of applying for a credit card at the same time as opening their account. However, as a foreign resident without a prior credit history in Japan, you may find you have difficulty obtaining a card. There are cases were a Japanese card issuer will accept a reference from an issuer whose card you have used in your own country. Most card issuers are reluctant to give their consent to the use of a foreign reference over the telephone, so if you really find yourself needing a credit card, your best bet is to apply by post, then wait and see.

Looking after your savings

After your first few months in Japan, when all the major expenses of getting set up in the country are behind you, your salary should leave you with a surplus at the end of every month. As rates of interest accruing on savings in Japan are invariably low, and always worst for current accounts, it would be wise to find the best way to invest these savings for a higher return.

Company savings schemes

If the company you work for operates a savings scheme, this could be the best place for you to deposit your savings. Company schemes are run for the benefit of employees and are usually organised on a no fee basis. This means that a company savings scheme can offer better returns than just about any financial institution.

Bank deposits

Every Japanese bank operates a number of savings accounts. The varying terms and conditions of these accounts are not much different to those available in the UK or any other Western country, meaning that the longer you commit your savings and the more you commit, the higher the return you can earn. Current examples of interest rates range from 1.28 per cent net for less than 3 million yen invested for a minimum of three months to 2.4 per cent net for more than 3 million invested for a minimum of four years.

Post Office schemes

As in the UK, the Japanese Post Office, or *yubin kyoku*, competes with banks and other financial institutions for savings. Compared to the banks, variations in interest rates are only marginal.

Securities companies

Japanese finance houses such as Nomura Shoken offer competitive rates of interest and probably represent the next best option to a company savings scheme. There are several schemes available but one that may be of interest to foreign residents is the one month deposit account offered by most companies. These accounts pay a return of 1.6-1.7 per cent net but their advantage is that your savings are only committed for one month at a time making things a lot more flexible.

All the Japanese daily papers feature details of savings accounts available with banks, the Post Office and other financial institutions. Get a Japanese friend to help you find where you can find the best home for your money.

KEEPING TABS ON YOUR TAXATION

No matter where you are and what you are doing, it is always wise to keep your tax affairs well ordered and living in Japan is no exception.

The income tax system

Japanese income tax, or *shotoku-zei* is based on a progressive system. The rates and tax bands are as listed in Fig. 14.

Tax band	Rate	Tax exempt allowance
1,000-2,999,000 yen	10%	0
3,000,000-5,999,000 yen	20%	300,000
6,000,000-9,999,000 yen	30%	900,000
10,000,000-19,999,000 yen	40%	1,900,000
Over 20,000,000 yen	50%	3,900,000

Fig. 14. Japanese income tax rates and allowances.

Pensions and welfare contributions

Pension contributions, or *kou-sei nenkin* are paid by all salary earners in Japan. The level of contributions is variable at between 2 and 6 per cent. However, as the chances of your deciding to take Japanese nationality are slim, *kou-sei nenkin* deductions from your salary represent a waste of your earnings as you will never be able to claim any benefits under the Japanese system. It is therefore, in your interests to opt out of the system. The Japanese have a far fairer attitude to the treatment of the earnings of foreign residents than the UK or the USA and it is possible in Japan to opt out. It should be noted however, that your employer (if he or she is Japanese and does not have much experience of administering taxation for *gaigin* staff) may take some persuading that this is in fact possible. Nevertheless, as the payment of this benefit over one or two years can add up to a substantial amount of money, it is in your best interests to insure that your earnings are protected.

Unemployment insurance, or *koyou hoken*, is another contribution paid from your salary for which you will gain no benefit. Unfortunately, at present, every earner is obliged to pay this contribution. The one positive point is that *koyou hoken* contributions at only 0.5 per cent of salary, take a relatively small slice from your earnings. A typical Japanese pay slip and translation is shown in Fig. 15.

Health insurance

Health insurance, or *kenko hoken*, is one contribution you would be well advised to pay rather than opt out. The cost of health care in Japan is very high, particularly if you have the misfortune to suffer an illness or accident requiring prolonged hospitalisation. Payable at a rate of approximately 4 per cent of earnings depending on salary level, *kenko hoken* cannot be called a negligible amount, but is worth paying considering the benefits:

Doctors', dentists' and chemists' fees

With an insurance card, issued on the payment of your first contribution, you will be obliged to pay only 10 per cent of the treatment received. Similarly, any prescription will be charged to you at 10 per cent of the actual cost, the remaining 90 per cent being paid through the *kenko hoken* system. As in other countries where a government system of health care exists, treatments such as cosmetic surgery and special dental treatments are not covered under the *kenko hoken* scheme.

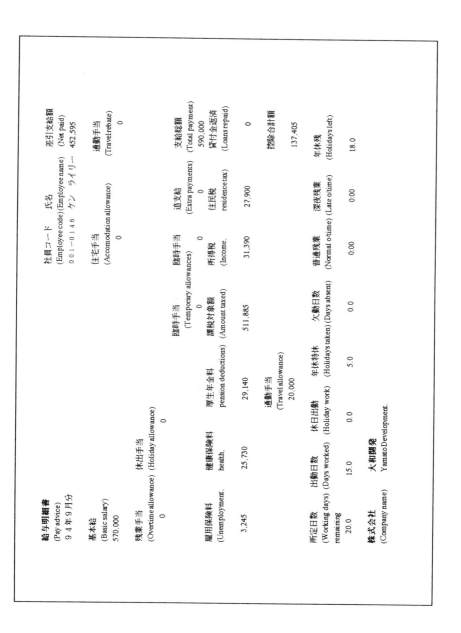

Fig. 15. Sample Japanese pay slip and translation.

Dependants

If you have any dependants who do not contribute directly into the *kenko hoken* system, they will be able to use your insurance, but the charges payable by them will be 30 per cent not 10 per cent.

Asking questions first

The *kenko hoken* system in Japan is not universal, in that some doctors and dentists refuse to treat patients who wish to claim treatment through their health insurance. To avoid any nasty shocks on completion of your treatment, it is always best to ask first whether the doctor or dentist you wish to treat you will accept payment via the *kenko hoken* system.

Other taxes

The taxes described thus far are withdrawn from salary at source. There is one other tax which you will be liable, residence tax, or *ju-min zei*, which can be deducted at source or paid by the tax payer directly, according to the individual's discretion.

Ju-min zei is a Japanese equivalent of the UK community charge and as such is a local tax paid at city or ward office level. The tax is based on the individual's earnings in the previous year. This means that a *gaigin* will be exempted from paying *ju-min zei* during his/her first year of residence in Japan. During the second year of residence, *ju-min zei* will be charged on the first year's earnings at a rate of between 5 and 15 per cent depending on the level of income and the city in which you reside.

If the individual chooses to pay *ju-min zei* directly rather than have it withdrawn from his/her salary, there are two alternative means of payment. Either the whole amount can be paid in one lump sum or payment can be split into four quarterly shares, interest accrues on any late payments.

10
A Few Last Words about the Language

No matter how short your planned stay in Japan (and bear in mind that most people end up staying longer than they had originally anticipated) learning at least the rudiments of the language is not only a courtesy to the Japanese, but also an invaluable aid to getting the most out of your stay. Many people who come to Japan and do not bother to study the language point out that it is difficult for someone brought up speaking a Western language to learn an Asian tongue. In fact, most Westerners who make the effort, realise that everyday Japanese is no difficult to learn for an English speaker than everyday French or German. One aspect of Japanese that does make life easier for foreign learners is the large number of foreign 'loan' words in common use in the Japanese language, a few examples of which are provided below. You should note that the Japanese do convert these loan words in their own system of pronunciation.

English	Japanese
Bread	Pan
Hamburger	Hamburger
Jeans	G-pan
Shirt	Shirts
Apartment	Apaa-to
Mansion	Mansion
Part-time job	Arbeito
Computer	Computa-

Television	Terebi
Coffee	Ko-hi

Written Japanese comprises three elements: Chinese characters, known as *kanji* and two syllables, known at *hiragana* and *katakana* each containing forty six symbols. *Katakana* is used principally for writing foreign loan words and as such can be an invaluable aid to finding your way around in your new Japanese environment. A day of study from one of several good basic Japanese language books available from bookshops and libraries, followed up by some spells of brief revision in the weeks prior to your journey to Japan would certainly help you make sense of your surroundings.

The 46 *katakana* symbols are shown in Fig. 16. together with their pronunciations. One important thing to note is that all Japanese syllables end with a vowel sound, so for example, the English word hamburger becomes *ha-mu-ba-ga* when pronounced in Japanese. Similarly, the English word orange becomes *oren-ji* when spoken in Japanese. The one exception to this rule are words which end with an -nn sound, such as mansion, which becomes *man-shi-on*. Some further examples of English loan words translated into *katakana* are shown in Fig. 17. The more you learn about *katakana*, the more you will realise that deciphering the Japanese pronunciations of foreign loan words is, like living in Japan, an intriguing, rewarding and often amusing experience.

ン	ワ	ラ	ヤ	マ	ハ	ナ	タ	サ	カ	ア
UN	WA	RA	YA	MA	HA	NA	TA	SA	KA	A

リ		ミ	ヒ	ニ	チ	シ	キ	イ
RI		MI	HI	NI	CHI	SHI	KI	I

ル	ユ	ム	フ	ヌ	ツ	ス	ク	ウ
RU	YU	MU	FU	NU	TSU	SU	KU	U

レ		メ	ヘ	ネ	テ	セ	ケ	エ
RE		ME	HE	NE	TE	SE	KE	E

ロ	ヨ	モ	ホ	ノ	ト	ソ	コ	オ
RO	YO	MO	HO	NO	TO	SO	KO	O

Mansion	マンション	Bread	パン
Computer	コンピュター	Shirt	シャツ
Coffee	コーヒ	Beer	ビール
America	アメリカ	France	フランス

Fig. 16. The *katakana* and English loan words translated into *katakana*.

案内書	Annai-sho	Brochure or pamphlet, (in this case a company brochure)
アルバイト	Arubeito	Part time work, (loan word, orginally German)
弁護士事務所	Bengoshi jimusho	Law firm
部長	Bu-cho	General manager
中華料理屋	Chuka ryori-ya	Chinese restaurant
英語	Eigo	English language
英会話	Eikai-wa	English conversation
不動産屋	Fudou-san-ya	Real estate agent
風呂	Furo	Japanese style bath
外圧	Gai-atsu	Political pressure from a foreign country
外人	Gai-gin	Foreigner
頑張って	Ganbatte	Try hard, do your best
判子	Hanko	Name stamp
法務所	Houmu-sho	Ministry of Justice
保証書	Hou-sho-sho	Letter of guarantee
住民税	Ju-min-zei	Residence tax
課長	Ka-cho	Manager
会社	Kaisha	Company
各駅停車	Kaku-eki-teisha	Slow train (stopping at all stations)
漢字	Kaniji	Chinese characters
契約書	Kei-yaku-sho	Contract

Fig. 17. (1 of 3) Japanese words used in this book.

健康保険	Kenko hoken	Health insurance
喫茶店	Kissa-ten	Cafe
コネ	Kone	Connections
厚生年金	Kousei nenkin	Pension
雇用保険	Koyou hoken	Unemployment insurance
区役所	Ku-yaku-sho	Ward office
給与保証書	Kyu-yo hou-sho-sho	Certificate guaranteeing income
面倒臭い	Mendou-kusai	Troublesome
南向け	Minami muke	Southern facing
水商売	Mizu-shoubai	The water trade
野税証明書	Nozei-shoumei-sho	Company tax certificate
らめん屋	Ramen-ya	Japanese noodle restaurant
冷房	Rei-bou	Air cooler
冷暖房	Rei-dan-bou	Air conditioner (hot & cold)
礼金	Rei-kin	'Thank you' money
履歴書	Ri-reki-sho	CV
正社員	Sei-sha-in	Permanent employee
敷金	Shiki-kin	Deposit
市役所	Shi-yaku-sho	City hall
食卓	Shoku-taku	Contract worker
所得税	Shotoku-zei	Income tax

Fig. 17. (2 of 3) Japanese words used in this book.

商社	Sho-sha	Trading company
手数料	Te-su-ryou	Commission
梅雨	Tsuyu	Rainy season
和風	Wa-fu	Japanese style
洋風	You-fu	Western style
郵便局	Yubin kyoku	Post office

Fig. 17. (3 of 3) Japanese words used in this book.

Appendix:
Useful Addresses

SPECIALIST JAPANESE RECRUITMENT SERVICES IN THE UK

Anglo Japanese Agency, 2nd Floor, Wormwood Chambers, 23/24
   Wormwood St, London EC2M 1RQ. Tel: (0171) 256 9371.
Cannon Persona International Recruitment, Aldermary House, 10-15
   Jewry, London EC3R 8AB. Tel: (0171) 489 8141.
JAC Recruitment, Dauntsey House, 3rd Floor, Fredericks Place, Old
   Jewry, London EC3R 8AB. Tel: (0171) 796 3132.
Japan Recruitment, 5 Sherwood St, London W1V 7RA.
   Tel: (0171) 734 442.

NB Selection Japan, 54 Jermyn St, London SW1Y 6LX.

EMPLOYMENT AGENCIES DEALING WITH FOREIGNERS IN JAPAN

Able Corporation, Otemachi 2-3-6, Chiyoda-ku, Tokyo 100, Japan.
   Tel: 03 3242 6506.
Advanced Management Associates, 305 Green Plaza, Nishi-Gotanda 8-
   5-1, Shinagawa-ku, Tokyo, 141, Japan. Tel: 03 3490 5877.
Beststaff Japan, Yoyogi 1-31-15, Shibuya-ku, Tokyo 151, Japan.
   Tel: 03 3379 7631.
Borgnan Human Development Institute, Daisan Taihei Bldg, Higashi-
   Ikebukuro 1-25-3, Toshima-ku, Toyko 170, Japan.
   Tel: 03 3989 8153.

MAJOR JAPANESE COMPANIES OPERATING IN THE UK
Banking and finance
Cosmo Securities Europe Ltd., 1st Floor, Garden House, 18 Finsbury
   Circus, London EC2M 7BP. Tel: (0171) 588 6733.
Dai-Ichi Kangyo Bank Ltd., DKB House, 24 King William St, London
   EC4R 9DB. Tel: (0171) 929 3319.

Daito Securities Co. Ltd., 74/78 Finsbury Pavement, London EC2A 1AT.
Tel: (0171) 638 7074.

Daiwa Bank Ltd., PO Box 70, Commercial Union Bldg, St. Helen's, 1
Undershaft, London EC3A 8JJ. Tel: (0171) 623 8200.

Diawa Europe Bank PLC., City Tower, 40 Basinghall St, London EC2V
5DE. Tel: (0171) 782 0875.

Ex-Im Bank of Japan, River Plate House, 7/11 Finsbury Circus, London
EC2M 7EX. Tel: (0171) 638 0175.

The Fuji Bank Ltd., River Plate House, 7/11 Finsbury Circus, London
EC2M 7DH. Tel: (0171) 588 2211.

Industrial Bank of Japan Ltd., Bucklersbury House, Walbrook, London
EC4N 8BR. Tel: (0171) 236 3266.

The Bank of Japan, 27/32 Old Jewry, London EC2R 8EY.
Tel: (0171) 606 2454.

Japan Development Bank, Level 4, City Tower, 40 Basinghall St, London
EC2V 5DE. Tel: (0171) 638 6210.

Kokusai Europe Ltd, 3rd & 4th Floors, 52/54 Gracechurch St, London
EC3 0EH. Tel: (0171) 626 2291.

Kyowa Saitama Bank Ltd., 30 Cannon St, London EC4M 6XH.
Tel: (0171) 248 7000.

Long Term Credit Bank of Japan, 18 King William St, London EC4N
7BR. Tel: (0171) 629 9217.

Maruman Securities Europe Ltd., 1 Liverpool St, London EC2M 7NH.
Tel: (0171) 382 9143.

Mitsubishi Bank, 6 Broadgate, London EC2M 2SX. Tel: (0171) 638 2222.

Mitsubishi Trust & Banking Corp., Mitsubishi Trust House, 24 Lombard
St, London EC3V 9AJ. Tel: (0171) 929 2323.

Mitsui Trust & Banking Co., 5F, 6 Broadgate, London EC2M 2TB.
Tel: (0171) 638 0841.

Nikko Securities Co. (Europe) Ltd., 55 Victoria St, London SW1H 0EU.
Tel: (0171) 799 2222.

Nippon Credit Bank Ltd., City Tower, 40 Basinghall St, London EC2V
5DE. Tel: (0171) 638 3460.

Nomura Bank International PLC./Nomura International Ltd., 1 St.
Martin's-le-Grand, London EC1A 4NP. Tel: (0171) 929 2366.

Sanwa International PLC., PO Box 245, Commercial Union Bldg, 1
Undershaft, London EC3A 8LA. Tel: (0171) 283 5252.

Sumitomo Bank Ltd., Temple Court, 11 Queen Victoria St, London
EC4N 4TA. Tel: (0171) 971 1000.

Sumitomo Finance International, 107 Cheapside, London EC2V 6DT.
Tel: (0171) 606 3001.

Sumitomo Trust & Banking Co., 155 Bishopgate, London EC2M 3XU. Tel: (0171) 945 7000.
Bank of Tokyo Ltd., Northgate House, 20/24 Moorgate, London EC2R 6DH. Tel: (0171) 638 1271.
Tokyo Securities Co. (Europe) Ltd., 1 London Wall Bldgs, London Wall, London EC2M 5PP. Tel: (0171) 248 9600.
Wako International (Europe) Ltd., Level 4, 155 Bishopsgate, London EC2M 3YX. Tel: (0171) 374 6055.
Yamaichi Bank (UK) PLC., Guildhall House, 81/87 Gresham St, London EC43V 7NQ. Tel: (0171) 600 1188.
Yasuda Trust & Banking Co., Ltd, 1 Liverpool St, London EC2M 7NH. Tel: (0171) 628 5721.

Trading companies
Chugai Boeki (UK) Ltd., Computer House, 6 Garrick Industrial Centre, Garrick Road, London NW9 6AQ. Tel: (0181) 202 3434.
Fuji Trading Co., 25 Queen Anne's Gate, London SW1H 9BU. Tel: (0171) 222 3171.
C.Itoh (UK) PLC., 76 Shoe Lane, London EC4A 3JB. Tel: (0171) 822 0822.
Kanematsu (UK) Ltd., Moor House, 119 London Wall, London EC2Y 5HX. Tel: (0171) 628 7901.
Marubeni UK PLC., New London Bridge House, London Bridge St, London SE1 9SW. Tel: (0171) 826 8600.
Meiji Seika Kaisha Ltd., Salisbury House, Finsbury Circus, London EC2M 5QQ. Tel: (0171) 638 2283.
Mitsubishi Corporation (UK) Ltd./Mitsubishi Euro-Africa S.A., Bow Bells House, Bread St, London EC4M 9BQ. Tel: (0171) 822 0022.
Mitsui & Co. Europe Ltd., 20 Old Bailey, London EC4M 7QQ. Tel: (0171) 822 0321.
Nichimen (Europe) BV., Latham House, 16 Minories, London EC3N 1EY. Tel: (0171) 480 6600.
Nissho Iwai (UK) Ltd., Bastion House, 140 London Wall, London EC2Y 5JT. Tel: (0171) 628 6030.
Nozaki Europe Ltd., 21/26 Garlick Hill, London EC4 2AU. Tel: (0171) 628 6030.
Okura & Co. UK Ltd., 40 Duke's Place, London EC3A 7LP. Tel: (0171) 283 2751.
Sumitomo Corporation (UK) Ltd., 107 Cheapside, London EC2V 6DQ. Tel: (0171) 220 9000.

Tomen (UK) Ltd., 13 Charles II St, London SW1 4QT.
Tel: (0171) 976 1255.

Toshoku Ltd., 14th Floor, St. Alphage House, 2 Fore St, London EC2Y
5DJ. Tel: (0171) 628 5481.

Electronics

Aiwa (UK) Ltd., Unit 5, Heathrow Summit Centre, Skyport Drive, West
Drayton, Middlesex UB7 0LY. Tel: (0181) 897 7000.

Apricot Electronics Ltd., 3500 Parkside, Birmingham Business Park,
Birmingham B37 7YS. Tel: (0121) 717 7171.

Brother Industries (UK) Ltd., Wrexham Technology Park, Croesnewydd
Road, Wrexham, Clwyd LL11 3BN. Tel: (01978) 821881.

Canon (UK) Ltd., Canon House, Manor Rd, Wallington, Surrey SM6
0AJ. Tel: (0181) 773 3173.

Casio Electronics Co. Ltd., Unit 6, 1000 North Circular Rd, London
NW2 7JD. Tel: (0181) 450 9131.

Citizen (Europe) Ltd., Wellington House, 4/10 Cowley Rd, Uxbridge,
Middlesex UB8 2XW. Tel: (01895) 72621.

Epson (UK) Ltd., Campus 100, Maylands Avenue, Hemel Hempstead,
Hertfordshire HP2 7EZ. Tel: (01442) 61144.

Fuji Electric (UK) Ltd., 40 George St, London W1H 5RE.
Tel: (0171) 935 0544.

Fujitsu (Europe) Ltd., 2 Longwalk Rd, Stockley Park, Uxbridge,
Middlesex UB11 1AB. Tel: (0181) 573 4444.

Funai Electric (UK) Ltd., Unit 14, Campfield Rd, Shoeburyness, Essex
SS3 9BZ. Tel: (01702) 2948111.

Hitachi Consumer Products, Hiwaun Industrial Estate, Aberdare, Mid
Glamorgan CF44 9UY. Tel: (01685) 811451.

Hitachi Denshi (UK) Ltd., 13/14 Garrick Industrial Centre, Irving Way,
Hendon, London NW9 6AQ. Tel: (0181) 202 4311.

Hitachi (Europe) Ltd., Whitebrook Park, Lower Cookham Road,
Maidenhead, Berks SL6 8YA. Tel: (01628) 585000.

JVC (UK) Ltd., JVC House, Eldonwall Trading Estate, Priestley Way,
London NW2 7BA. Tel: (0181) 450 3282.

Konica UK Ltd., Plane Tree Crescent, Feltham, Middlesex TW13 7HD.
Tel: (0181) 751 6121.

Matsushita Electric (UK) Ltd., Pentwyn Industrial Estate, Cardiff CF2
7XB. Tel: (01222) 731761.

Maxwell (UK) Ltd., 3A High Street, Rickmansworth, Hertfordshire
WD3 1HR. Tel: (01923) 777171.

Minolta (UK) Ltd., 1/9 Tanners Drive, Blakelands North, Milton Keynes
MK14 5BU. Tel: (01908) 211211.

Mitsubishi Electric (UK) Ltd., Travellers Lane, Hatfield, Hertfordshire AL10 8XB. Tel: (01707) 276100.

NEC (UK) Ltd., NEC House, 1 Victoria Rd, London W3 6UL. Tel: (0181) 993 8111.

Oki Electric Industry Co. Ltd., Ground Floor North, 3 Shortlands, Hammersmith International Centre, London W6 8BT. Tel: (0181) 741 2324.

Olympus Optical Co. (UK) Ltd., 2/8 Honduras St, London EC1Y 0TX. Tel: (0171) 253 2772.

Panasonic Europe (HQ) Ltd., Panasonic House, Willoughby Rd, Bracknell, Berks RG12 4FP. Tel: (01344) 853901.

Pentax UK Ltd., Pentax House, South Hill Avenue, South Harrow, Middlesex HA2 0LT. Tel: (0181) 864 4422.

Pioneer High Fidelity (GB) Ltd., Field Way, Greenford, Middlesex UB6 8UZ. Tel: (0181) 575 5757.

Ricoh UK Ltd., Ricoh House, 1 Plane Tree Crescent, Feltham, Middlesex TW13 7HG. Tel: (0181) 571 6611.

Sanyo Electric Co. Ltd., Unit BT 50/1 Sadler Forster Way, Teeside Industrial Estate, Thornaby, Cleveland TS17 9JY. Tel: (01642) 750340.

Seikosha (UK) Ltd., Unit 14, Newlands Drive, Colnbrook, Slough, Berks SL3 0DX. Tel: (01753) 685873.

Sharp Electronics (UK) Ltd., Thorp Road, Newton Heath, Manchester M10 9BE. Tel: (0161) 205 2333.

Sony (UK) Ltd., Sony House, South St, Staines, Middlesex TW18 4PF. Tel: (01784) 467000.

TDK UK Ltd., TDK House, 5/7 Queensway, Redhill RH1 1YB. Tel: (01737) 773773.

Toshiba Corporation Europe, Audrey House, Ely Place, London EC1N 6SN. Tel: (0171) 242 7295.

Yamaha Electronics (UK) Ltd., 200 Rickmansworth Rd, Watford, Hertfordshire WD1 8EB. Tel: (01923) 816444.

Automotive

Bridgestone Tyre UK Ltd., Birchley Trading Estate, Oldbury, Warley, West Midlands B69 1DT. Tel: (0121) 552 3331.

Daihatsu (UK) Ltd., Poulton Close, Dover, Kent CT17 0HP. Tel: (01304) 213030.

Honda Motor Europe Ltd., 4 Power Rd, Chiswick, London W4 5YT. Tel: (0181) 747 1400.

IBC Vehicles Ltd., PO Box 163, Kimpton Rd, Luton LU2 0TY. Tel: (01502) 426302.

Kawasaki Motors UK Ltd., 1 Dukes Meadow, Millboard Rd, Bourne End, Bucks SL6 5XG. Tel: (01628) 851000.

Mazda Cars (UK) Ltd., 77 Mount Ephraim, Tunbridge Wells, Kent TN4 8BS. Tel: (01892) 511877.

Nippondenso International (UK) Ltd., Roycraft House, 15 Linton Rd, Barking, Essex IG11 8HG. Tel: (0181) 591 9050.

Nissan Europe N.V. (London), 5 Arlington St, St. Jame's, London SW1A 1RA. Tel: (0171) 409 7988.

Subaru (UK) Ltd., Ryder St, West Bromwich, West Midlands B70 0EJ. Tel: (0121) 522 2000.

Suzuki GB Cars Ltd., 46/62 Gatwick Rd, Crawley, West Sussex RH10 2XF. Tel: (01293) 518000.

Toyota (GB) Ltd., The Quadrangle, Redhill, Surrey RH1 1PX. Tel: (01737) 768585.

Heavy industry

Daihatsu Diesel (Europe) Ltd., Suite 15, Beaufort Court, Admirals Way, London E14 9KL. Tel: (0171) 538 5387.

Fuji Industries Co. Ltd., 197 Knightsbridge, London SW7 1RB. Tel: (0171) 581 5111.

Hitachi Construction Machinery, Europe Liaison Office, 36 Castlefield Industrial Estate, Bridgewater, Somerset TA6 4DH. Tel: (01278) 425533.

Ishikawajima Harima Heavy Industries Co. Ltd., Europe House, World Trade Centre, London E1 9AA. Tel: (0171) 626 1010.

Kawasaki Heavy Industrial (UK) Ltd., 3 St. Helen's Place, 4th Floor, London EC3A 6EB. Tel: (0171) 628 9915.

Kobe Steel Europe Ltd., Alton House, 174/177 High Holborn, London WC1V 7AA. Tel: (0171) 836 1225.

Komatsu (UK) Ltd., Durham Rd, Birtley Chester le Street, Co. Durham DH3 2QX. Tel: (0191) 271 1616.

Kubota Corporation, 11/12 Hanover St, London W1R 9HF. Tel: (0171) 629 6471.

Mitsubishi Heavy Industries Europe Ltd., Bow Bells House, Bread St, London EC4M 9BQ. Tel: (0171) 248 8821.

Mitsui Engineering & Shipbuilding Co. Ltd., 14th Floor, St. Alphage House, 2 Fore St, London EC2Y 5DA. Tel: (0171) 588 9277.

NKK (UK) Ltd., 4th Floor, West Block, 11 Moorfields High Walk, London EC2Y 9DE. Tel: (0171) 628 2161.

Sharp Precision Manufacturing (UK) Ltd., Forward House, Davy Way, Llay, Wrexham, Clwyd LL12 0PG. Tel: (01978) 856441.

Sumitomo Heavy Industries (Europe) Ltd., Ibex House, 42/47 Minories, London EC3N 1D7. Tel: (0171) 702 1221.

Construction/civil engineering

Aoki Corporation, Suite 22, Ivor House, Bridge Street, Cardiff CF1 2TH. Tel: (01222) 665596.

Kajima Corporation (EHQ), Grove House, 248A Marylebone Rd, London NW1 6JZ. Tel: (0171) 465 0007.

Kumagai-Gumi Co. Ltd., 8 St. Jame's Square, London SW1Y 4JU. Tel: (0171) 925 0066.

Mitsui Construction Co. Ltd., 1F, 6/8 Sackville Street, London W1X 1DD. Tel: (0171) 287 2520.

Ohbayashi Europe BV/Obayashi Properties (UK) Ltd., 2nd Floor, Old Burlington St, London W1X 1LB. Tel: (0171) 434 9595.

Shimizu Corporation, 110 St. Martin's Lane, London WC2N 4PJ. Tel: (0171) 930 1873.

Taisei Europe Ltd (EHQ), 3 Hanover Square, London W1R 9RD. Tel: (0171) 629 9701.

Takenaka (UK) Ltd., Tavistock House South, Tavistock Square, London WC1H 9LG. Tel: (0171) 383 0956.

Chemicals/pharmaceuticals

Ajinomoto Co. Ltd., 2nd Floor, 18 Grosvenor Street, London W1X 9FD. Tel: (0171) 493 7790.

Asahi Chemical Industry Co. Ltd., (Liaison Office), 54 Grosvenor Street, London W1X 9FH. Tel: (0171) 493 3583.

Chugai Pharmaceutical Co. Ltd., Mulliner House, Flanders Road, Turnham Green, London W4 1NN. Tel: (0181) 747 4656.

Fujisawa Pharmaceutical Co. Ltd., 2nd Floor, Albany House, 180 Albany St, London NW1 4AW. Tel: (0171) 387 3751.

Idemitsu Petrochemical Co. Ltd., 2nd Floor, Nightingale House, 65 Curzon St, London W1Y 7PE. Tel: (0171) 629 9615.

Kanebo Cosmetics UK Ltd., Bone Lane, Newbury, Berks RG14 5TD. Tel: (01635) 46362.

Kansai Paint Co. Ltd., Bastion House, 140 London Wall, London EC2Y 5JT. Tel: (0171) 628 8713.

Mitsubishi Kasei (UK) PLC., 22 City Road, London EC1Y 2AJ. Tel: (0171) 588 1810.

Mitsubishi Petrochemical Co. Ltd., 3rd Floor Bow Bells House, Bread Street, London EC4M 9BQ. Tel: (0171) 248 0862.

Mitsui Petrochemical Industries Europe Ltd., 20 Old Bailey, London EC4M 7QQ. Tel: (0171) 236 2463.

Mitsui Pharmaceuticals Inc., 13 Charles II Street, London SW1Y 4QU.
Tel: (0171) 976 1184.
Nippon Paint (Europe) Ltd., Level 8, City Tower, 40 Basinghall Street,
London EC2V 5DE. Tel: (0171) 628 4667.
Otsuka Chemical Co. Ltd., 6th Floor, Roman House, Wood Street,
London EC2Y 5BA. Tel: (0171) 638 8262.
Otsuka Pharmaceutical Co. Ltd., Otsuka House, 322 King Street,
Hammersmith, London W6 0RR. Tel: (01781) 748 8783.
Shiseido UK Ltd., Ivory Place, Treadgold Street, London W11 4BT.
Tel: (0171) 792 1575.

JAPANESE ASSOCIATIONS AND FOUNDATIONS IN THE UK

Anglo-Japanese Economic Institute, Rooms 1/6, Morley House,
314/322 Regent Street, London W1R 5AD. Tel: (0171) 637 7872.
Datwa Anglo-Japanese Foundation, 55 King William Street, London
EC4N 7AX. Tel: (0171) 822 3803.
Electronic Industries Association of Japan, 1 Dean's Yard, Westminster,
London SW1P 3NR. Tel: (0171) 799 9811.
Euro-Japanese Exchange Foundation, EJEF Study Centre, Lane End,
High Wycombe, Bucks HP14 3HH. Tel: (01494) 882091.
Euro-Japanese Foundation, 5th Floor, Portland House, 4 Great Portland
Street, London W1N 5AA. Tel: (0171) 436 0588.
The Japan Association, Swire House, 59 Buckingham Gate, London
SW1E 6AJ. Tel: (0171) 821 3220.
Japan Centre for International Finance (JCIF), 11th Floor, Bucklersbury
House, 83 Cannon Street, London EC4N 8EJ. Tel: (0171) 236 1502.
Japanese Chamber of Commerce and Industry in the UK, 2nd Floor,
Salisbury House, 29 Finsbury Circus, London EC2M 5QQ.
Tel: (0171) 628 0069.
The Japan Foundation, 35 Dover Street, London W1X 3RA.
Tel: (0171) 499 4726.
Miura Anjinkai (The Will Adams Association), 75 Kenton Street,
London NW1. Tel: (0171) 278 0926.

SPECIALIST JAPANESE RECRUITMENT SERVICES IN THE UK

Anglo Japanese Agency, 2nd Floor, Wormwood Chambers, 23/24
Wormwood St, London EC2M 1RQ. Tel: (0171) 256 9371.
Cannon Persona International Recruitment, Aldermary House, 10-15
Queen St, London EC4N 1TX. Tel: (0171) 489 8141.

JAC Recruitment, Dauntsey House, 3rd Floor, Fredericks Place, Old
  Jewry, London EC3R 8AB. Tel: (0171) 796 3132.
Japan Recruitment, 5 Sherwood St, London W1V 7RA.
  Tel: (0171) 734 442.

NB Selection Japan, 54 Jermyn St, London SW1Y 6LX.

JAPANESE GOVERNMENT OFFICES

UK

Consulate General of Japan, 2 Melville Crescent, Edinburgh EH3 7HW.
Tel: (0131) 225 4777.
Embassy of Japan, 101-104 Piccadilly, London W1V 9FN.
  Tel: (0171) 465 6500.
Japan External Trade Organisation (JETRO), 6th Floor, Leconfield
  House, Curzon St, London W1Y 7FB. Tel: (0171) 493 7226.
Japan National Trust Office (JNTO), 167 Regent St, London W1.
  Tel: (0171) 734 9638.

Ireland

Embassy of Japan, Nutley Bldg, Merrion Centre, Nutley Lane, Dublin 4.
Japan External Trade Organisation (JETRO), 1 Setanta Place, Dublin 2.
  Tel: (01) 671 4003.

USA

Consulate General of Japan, # 701, 550 W. 7th Avenue, Anchorage,
Alaska. Tel: (907) 279 8428.
    # 1507, 250 E. 1st St, Los Angeles.
     California. Tel: (213) 624 8305.
    299 Park Avenue, New York City.
     New York 10171. Tel: (212) 371 8222.
    50 Fremont St, San Francisco.
     California 94105. Tel: (415) 777 3533.
    601 Union St, Seattle, Washington 8101.
     Tel: (206) 682 9107.

Embassy of Japan, 2520 Massachusetts Avenue, N.W., Washington D.C.
  2008. Tel: (202) 234 2266.
Japan External Trade Organisation (JETRO), 44F McGraw Hill Bldg,
  1221 Avenue of the Americas, New York, NY 10020-1060. Tel:
  (212) 997 0400.
    # 1890, 725 S. Figueroa St,
     Los Angeles CA 90017. Tel: (213) 624 8855.

#501 Quantas Bldg,
360 Post St, San Francisco, CA94108. Tel: (415) 392 1333.
Japan National Tourist Organisation (JNTO), Rockefeller Plaza, 630
Fifth Avenue, New York City, NY 10111. Tel: (212) 757 5640.
#2640, 624 S. Grand Avenue, Los Angeles CA 90017. Tel: (213)
623 1952.
Suite 601, 360 Post St, San Francisco, CA 94108. Tel: (415) 989 7140.

Australia
Consulate General of Japan, 3rd Floor, Holland House, 492 St. Kilda
Rd, Melbourne, Victoria 3004. Tel: (03) 867 349.
The Forrest Centre, 221 St. George's Terrace, Perth W.A.
Tel: (09) 312 7816.
Comalco Place, 12 Creek St, Brisbane, Queensland 4000.
Tel: 221 5188.
State Bank Centre, 52 Martin Place, Sydney N.S.W. 2000.
Tel: (02) 231 3455.
Embassy of Japan, 112 Empire Circuit, Yarralumla, Canberra, ACT
2600. Tel: 273 3244.
Japan External Trade Organisation (JETRO), 4F, Standard Chartered
House, 30 Collins St, Melbourne, Victoria 3000. Tel: (03) 654 4949.
8th Floor, St. George's Court Bdlg, 16 St. George's Terrace, Perth W.A.
6000. Tel: (09) 325 2809.
Level 19, Gateway 1, MacQuarrie Place, Sydney, N.S.W. 2000.
Tel: (02) 241 1181.
Japan National Tourist Organisation (JNTO), 115 Pitt St, Sydney
N.S.W. 2000. Tel: (02) 232 4522.

Canada
Embassy of Japan, 255 Sussex Drive, Ottawa, Ontario K1N 9E6.
Tel: (613) 236 8541.
Japan External Trade Organisation (JETRO), Place Montreal, Trust
Tower Suite 2902, 1800 McGill College Avenue, Montreal, Quebec
H3A 3J6. Tel: (514) 849 5911.
Suite 700 Brittanica House, 151 Floor West St, Toronto, Ontario M5S
1T7. Tel: (416) 962 5055.
Japan National Tourist Organisation (JNTO), 165 University Avenue,
Toronto, Ontario M5H 3BB. Tel: (416) 366 7140.
660 World Trade Centre, 999 Canada Place, Vancouver, British Columbia
V6C 3EI. Tel: (604) 684 4174.

New Zealand

Consulate General of Japan, National Mutual Centre Bldg, 37-45 Shortland St, Auckland 1, New Zealand. Tel: (09) 303 4106.

General Bldg, 77 Hereford Street, Christchurch 1, New Zealand. Tel: 665 680.

Embassy of Japan, Norwich Insurance House, 3-11 Hunter St, Wellington 1, New Zealand. Tel: 731 540.

Japan External Trade Organisation (JETRO), No 301 Dilworth Bldg, Customs St, East Auckland, New Zealand. Tel: (09) 379 7427.

EMPLOYMENT AGENCIES DEALING WITH FOREIGNERS IN JAPAN

Abel Corporation, 2-3-6 Otemachi, Chiyoda-ku, Tokyo 100. Tel: (03) 3242 6506.

Advanced Management Associates, 305 Green Plaza, 8-5-1 Nishi-Gotanda Shinagawa-ku, Tokyo 141. Tel: (03) 3490 5877.

Beststaff Japan, 1-31-15 Yoyogi, Shibuya-ku, Tokyo 151. Tel: (03) 3379 7631.

Borgnan Human Development Institute, Daisan Taihei Bldg, 1-25-3 Higashi-Ikebukuro, Toshima-ku, Tokyo 170. Tel: (03) 3989 8153.

Cambridge Corporation, 1-11-45 Akasaka, Minato-ku, Tokyo 107. Tel: (03) 3582 8931.

ECI Inc., Hibiya Kokusai Bldg, 2-2-3 Uchisaiwaicho, Chiyoda-ku, Tokyo 100. Tel: (03) 3593 0971.

Freelance Hands, 1-15-3 Dogenzaka, Shibuya-ku, Tokyo 150. Tel: (03) 3476 2142.

IIS Company, 2-15-3 Minami Aoyama, Minato-ku, Tokyo 107. Tel: (03) 3479 2826.

IMCA, Bungei Shunju Shinkan, 23 Kioi-cho, Chiyoda-ku, Tokyo 102. Tel: (03) 3221 9211.

JKC Recruiting, 4F Yamagata Bldg, 1-14-7 Shinbashi, Minato-ku, Tokyo 105. Tel: (03) 3502 3991.

Mega Consultants, 206 Mezondo Seki, 4-9-3 Yotsuya, Shinjuku-ku, Tokyo 160. Tel: (03) 3226 5701.

Nippon Manpower, 5F Akane Bldg, 4-1-31 Asasaka, Minato-ku, Tokyo 107. Tel: (03) 3224 0221.

Oak Associates, 504 Misawa Bldg, 5-21-5 Sendagaya, Shibuya-ku, Tokyo 151. Tel: (03) 3354 9502.

Technics in Management Transfer, 5F KK Bldg, 13-8 Ichiban-cho, Chiyoda-ku, Tokyo 102. Tel: (03) 3221 1011.

TMT/ABA, KK Bldg, 13-8 Ichiban-cho, Chiyoda-ku, Tokyo 102.
Tel: (03) 3221 1331.
Tokyo Executive Search Co., Kioicho TRB Bldg, 5-7 Koji-machi,
Chiyoda-ku, Tokyo 102. Tel: (03) 3230 1881.

ACCOUNTANTS EMPLOYING FOREIGNERS IN JAPAN

Arthur Andersen Japan, Nihon Seimei Bldg, 8-1-9 Akasaka, Minato-ku,
Tokyo 107. Tel: (03) 3403 4211.
Arthur Young/Asahi Shinwa, 4F Nissei Bldg, 1-18 Ageba-cho, Shinjuku-
ku, Tokyo 162. Tel: (03) 3235 8511.
Coopers & Lybrand/Chuo Audit Corp., 29F Kasumigaseki Bldg, 3-2-5
Kasumigaseki, Chiyoda-ku, Tokyo 100. Tel: (03) 3581 7535.
Deloitte, Haskins & Sells/Mita Audit Corp., Mita Kokusai Bldg, 1-4-28
Mita, Minato-ku, Tokyo 108. Tel: (03) 3454 1251.
Ernst & Whinney/Showa, Ota & Co., 2-2-3 Uchisaiwai-cho, Chiyoda-
ku, Tokyo 100. Tel: (03) 3503 1191.
Peat Marwick, Minato, 6F Nihon Sekijujisha Bldg, 1-1-3 Shiba
Daimon, Minato-ku, Tokyo 105. Tel: (03) 3403 2551.
Price Waterhouse/Aoyama Audit Corp., Aoyama Bldg, 1-2-3 Kita-
Aoyama, Minato-ku, Tokyo 107. Tel: (03) 3404 9351.
Touche Ross/Sanwa Tomatsu & Aoki, MS Shibaura Bldg, 4-13-23
Shibaura, Minato-ku, Tokyo 108. Tel: (03) 3457 1698.

ADVERTISING AGENCIES EMPLOYING FOREIGNERS IN JAPAN

Daiko Advertising, 4-3-39 Miyahara, Yodogawa-ku, Osaka 532.
Tel: (06) 392. 8301.
Dentsu Inc., 2-45 Dojima, Kita-ku, Osaka 530. Tel: (06) 342 2184.
Denstu Advertising, 1-11-10 Tsukiji, Chuo-ku, Tokyo 104.
Tel: (03) 3544 6666.
Hakuhodo Inc., 2-3-18 Nakanoshima, Kita-ku, Osaka 530.
Tel: (06) 228 4000.
Hakuhodo Inc., 3-22 Nishiki-cho, Chiyoda-ku, Tokyo 101.
Tel: (03) 3240 7777.
J. Walter Thompson, 1-4-10 Takanawa, Minato-ku, Tokyo.
Tel: (03) 3440 4848.
Kyodo Advertising, Hibiya Chunichi Bldg, 2-1-4 Uchisaisai-cho,
Chiyoda-ku, Tokyo 100. Tel: (03) 3503 1311.
Mannensha Inc., 1-16 Awaji-machi, Higashi-ku, Osaka 541.
Tel: (06) 202 2212.

McCann Erickson/Hakuhodo, 1-1-1 Minami- Aoyama, Minato-ku, Tokyo 107. Tel: (03) 3746 8247.

Naylor, Hara International, 1057 Shin Taisho Bldg, 2-10-7 Dogenzaka, Shibuya-ku, Tokyo 150. Tel: (03) 3463 2560.

Standard Advertising, Sumitomo, Higashi-Shinbashi Bldg, 1-1-11 Hamamatsu-cho, Minato-ku, Tokyo 100. Tel: (03) 3434 8181.

Tokyu Agency, 1-3-1-600 Umeda, Kita-ku, Osaka 530. Tel: (06) 344 3256.

Tokyu Agency, 4-8-18 Akasaka, Minato-ku, Tokyo 107. Tel: (03) 3404 5311.

ARCHITECTS AND CONSTRUCTION COMPANIES EMPLOYING FOREIGNERS IN JAPAN

Currie & Brown, Gosei Bldg, 5-16-17 Minami-Azabu, Minato-ku, Tokyo 106. Tel: (03) 3442 6642.

Daiwa Construction, 1-5-34 Bunkyo-ku, Tokyo 113. Tel: (03) 3812 7231.

Davy Corp. PLC., Shokin Bldg, 8-11-12 Ginza, Tokyo 104. Tel: (03) 3571 2297.

Fujita Corporation, 4-6-15 Sendagaya, Shibuya-ku, Tokyo 151. Tel: (03) 3402 1911.

Hasegawa Komuten, 2-32-1 Shiba, Minato-ku, Tokyo 151. Tel: (03) 3456 5451.

Kajima Construction, 1-2-7 Moto Akasaka, Minato-ku, Tokyo 107. Tel: (03) 3404 3311.

Komatsu Construction Co., 3-5-4 Shiba-Koen, Minato-ku, Tokyo 105. Tel: (03) 3434 5131.

Kumagai-Gumi, 1-2 Tskudo-cho, Shinjuku-ku, Tokyo 162. Tel: (03) 3260 2111.

Kume Architects & Engineers Co., 1-13-11 Nishi Azabu, Minato-ku, Tokyo 106. Tel: (03) 3404 0251.

Matsui Construction, 1-17-22 Shinkawa, Chuo-ku, Tokyo 104. Tel: (03) 3553 1152.

Mitsubishi Estate (Design Dept.), 2-4-11 Marunouchi, Chiyoda-ku, Tokyo 100. Tel: (03) 3287 5100.

Nikken, 2-1041-21 Ikebukuro, Toshima-ku, Tokyo 171. Tel: (03) 35992 3091.

Nikken Sekkei, 1-4-27 Koraku, Bunkyo-ku, Tokyo 112. Tel: (03) 3813 3361.

Obayashi Corporation, 2-3 Kanda Tsukasa-cho, Chiyoda-ku, Tokyo 101. Tel: (03) 3292 1111.

Sekki Design, Yamatane Bldg, 1-11-22 Minami Ikebukuro, Toshima-ku, Tokyo 171. Tel: (03) 3989 9511.

Shimizu Corporation, Kyobashi 2-16-1, Chuo-ku, Chiyoda-ku, Tokyo 101. Tel: (03) 3535 411.

Taisei Corporation, 1-25-1 Nishi Shinjuku, Shinjuku-ku, Tokyo 163. Tel: (03) 3348 1111.

Takenaka Corporation, 8-21-1 Ginza, Chuo-ku, Tokyo 104. Tel: (03) 3542 7100.

Toda Corporation, 1-7-1 Kyobashi, Chuo-ku, Tokyo 104. Tel: (03) 3562 6111.

BANKS AND SECURITIES HOUSE EMPLOYING FOREIGNERS IN JAPAN

Bankers Trust Company, Kishimoto Bldg, 2-1 marunouchi 2-chome, Chiyoda-ku, Tokyo. Tel: (03) 3286 0717.

Bank of Japan, 2-1-1 Hongoku-cho, Nihon bashi, Chuo-ku, Tokyo 103. Tel: (03) 3279 1111.

Bank of Nova Scotia, 21F Fukoku Seimei Bldg, 2-2 Uchisaiwaicho 2-chome, Chiyoda-ku, Tokyo 100. Tel: (03) 3593 0201.

Bank of Tokyo, PO Box 265, Shinjuku, Tokyo 163-91. Tel: (03) 3342 6513.

Baring Securities, 10F Shin Kasumigaseki Bldg, 3-3-2 Kasumigaseki, Chiyoda-ku, Tokyo 100. Tel: (03) 3595 8811.

Cosmo Securities, 1-16-10 Nihonbashi, Chuo-ku, Tokyo 103. Tel: (03) 3272 4611.

Chase Investment Bank, 1-2-1 Maurouchi, Chiyoda-ku, Tokyo 100. Tel: (03) 3287 4099.

Chase Manhatton Asia Ltd, 3-7-12 Toranomon, Minato-ku, Tokyo 105. Tel: (03) 3287 4104.

Citicorp/Citibank, 2-2-1 Otemachi, Chiyoda-ku, Tokyo 100. Tel: (03) 3273 6640.

Dai Ichi Kangyo Bank, 1-1-5 Uchisaiwai-cho, Chiyoda-ku, Tokyo 100. Tel: (03) 3596 1111.

Daiwa Securities, 2-6-4 Otemachi, Chiyoda-ku, Tokyo 100. Tel: (03) 3243 2111.

Drexel, Burnham, Lambert, 11F Imperial Tower, 1-1 Uchisaiwaicho 1-chome, Chiyoda-ku, Tokyo 100. Tel: (03) 3508 7801.

Kuji Bank, 1-5-5 Otemachi, Chiyoda-ku, Tokyo 100. Tel: (03) 3216 2211.

Hambros Bank Ltd, 5F Fukoku Seimei Bldg, 2-2-2 Uchisaiwai-cho, Chiyoda-ku, Tokyo 100. Tel: (03) 3508 2141.

Hill Samuel, Tokyo Representative Office, 6F Tokyo Shoyu Kaikan Bldg, 3-3-1 Kasumigaseki, Chiyoda-ku, Tokyo 100. Tel: (03) 3501 6491.

Industrial Bank of Japan, 3-3 Maronouchi 1-chome, Chiyoda-ku, Tokyo 100. Tel: (03) 3214 1111.

James Capel Pacific, 7F Kokusai Bldg, 3-1-1 Marunouchi, Chiyoda-ku, Tokyo 100. Tel: (03) 3282 0111.

J.P. Morgan, New Yurakucho Bldg, 12-1 Yurakucho 1-chrome, Chiyoda-ku, Tokyo 100. Tel: (03) 3282 0378.

Kleinwort Benson International Inc., 801 Kokusai Bldg, 3-1-1 Marunouchi, Chiyoda-ku, Tokyo 100. Tel: (03) 3218 0800.

Kokusai Securities, 2-27-1 Shinkawa, Chuo-ku, Tokyo 104. Tel: (03) 3297 2111.

Lloyds Bank PLC., Ote Centre Bldg, 1-1-3 Ohtemachi, Chiyoda-ku, Tokyo. Tel: (03) 3214 6771.

Midland Bank PLC., AIU Bldg, 1-1-3 Marunouchi, Chiyoda-ku, Tokyo 100. Tel: (03) 3284 1861.

Mitsubishi Bank, 2-7-1 Marunouchi, Chiyoda-ku, Tokyo 100. Tel: (03) 3240 1111.

Mitsubishi Trust & Banking, 1-4-5 Marunouchi, Chiyoda-ku, Tokyo 100. Tel: (03) 3212 1211.

Mitsui Bank, 1-1-2 Yurakucho, Chiyoda-ku, Tokyo 100. Tel: (03) 3270 9511.

National Westminster Bank PLC., AIU Bldg, 1-1-3 Marunouchi, Chiyoda-ku, Tokyo 100. Tel: (03) 3216 5301.

New Japan Securities, 3-11 Kanda Suragadai, Chiyoda-ku, Tokyo 101. Tel: (03) 3219 1111.

Nikko Securities, 1-6-1 Marunouchi, Chiyoda-ku, Tokyo 100. Tel: (03) 3283 2211.

Nippon Credit Bank, 13-10 Kudan-kita, 1-chrome, Chiyoda-ku, Tokyo 102. Tel: (03) 3263 1111.

Nippon Kangyo Kakumaru Securities, 1-6-1 Marunouchi, Chiyoda-ku, Tokyo 100. Tel: (03) 3286 7458.

Nomura, Babcock & Brown, 1-12-11 Nihonbashi, Chuo-ku, Tokyo 103. Tel: (03) 3281 7141.

Nomura Securities, 1-9-1 Nihonbashi, Chuo-ku, Tokyo 103. Tel: (03) 3211 1811.

Paine Webber Inc., AIU Bldg, 1-1-3 Marunouchi, Chiyoda-ku, Tokyo 100. Tel: (03) 3215 7264.

N.M. Rothschild & Sons, 4F AIU Bldg, 1-1-3 Marunouchi, Chiyoda-ku, Tokyo 100. Tel: (03) 3201 8601.

Royal Bank of Scotland PLC., Dai-Ichi Seimei Sogo Kan, 3-7-1 Kyobashi, Chuo-ku, Tokyo 104. Tel: (03) 3567 7078.

Saitama Bank, 1-2-6 Muromachi, Nihonbashi, Chuo-ku, Tokyo 103. Tel: (03) 3276 6662.

Sanwa Bank, 1-1-1 Otemachi, Chiyoda-ku, Tokyo 100. Tel: (03) 3216 3111.

Sanyo Securities, 1-8-1 Nihonbashi, Nihonbashi, Chuo-ku, Tokyo 103. Tel: (03) 3666 1233.

S.G. Warburg Securities (Japan) Inc., New Edobashi Bldg, 1-7-2 Nihonbashi Honcho, Chuo-ku, Tokyo 103. Tel: (03) 246 4111.

Schroders Securities (Japan) Ltd., 26F Ark Mori Bldg, 1-12-32, Akasaka, Minato-ku, Tokyo 107. Tel: (03) 5562 8800.

Standard Chartered Bank, Fuji Bldg, 3-2-3 Marunouchi, Chiyoda-ku, Tokyo 100. Tel: (03) 3213 6541.

Sumitomo Bank, 1-3-2 Marunouchi, Chiyoda-ku, Tokyo 100. Tel: (03) 3283 5111.

Sumitomo Trust & Banking, 1-4-4 Marunouchi, Chiyoda-ku, Tokyo 100. Tel: (03) 3286 1111.

Tokyo Forex Co., 2-15 Nihonbashi-koamicho, Chuo-ku, Tokyo 102. Tel: (03) 3270 8801.

Wako Securities, 6-1 Koami-cho, Nihonbashi, Chuo-ku, Tokyo 103.

Yamaichi Securities, Nihonbashi, 1-7 Kabuto-cho, Chuo-ku, Tokyo 104. Tel: (03) 3666 2281.

Yasuda Trust & Banking, 2-1 Yaesu 1-chome, Chuo-ku, Tokyo 103. Tel: (03) 3278 8111.

BUSINESS CONSULTANTS EMPLOYING FOREIGNERS IN JAPAN

Arthur D. Little, Fukido Bldg, 4-1-13 Toranomon, Minato-ku, Tokyo 105. Tel: (03) 3436 2196.

Booz. Allen & Hamilton, Imperial Tower Bldg, 1-1-1 Uchisaiwai-cho, Chiyoda-ku, Tokyo 100. Tel: (03) 3501 1922.

The Boston Consulting Group, Time Life Bldg, 2-3-6 Otemachi, Chiyoda-ku, Tokyo 100. Tel: (03) 3279 0761.

Dodwell Marketing, 8F Togin Bldg, 1-4-2 Marunouchi, Chiyoda-ku, Tokyo 100. Tel: (03) 3211 4451.

McKinsey & Co., Yamato Life Insurance Bldg, 1-1-7 Uchisaiwaicho, Chiyoda-ku, Tokyo 11. Tel: (03) 3581 5571.

Mitsubishi Research Institute, Time Life Bldg, 2-3-6 Otemachi, Chiyoda-ku, Tokyo 100. Tel: (03) 33270 8100.

NRI/NCC, Sumitomo Twin Bldg, 2-27-1 Shinkawa, Cho-ku, Tokyo 104. Tel: (03) 3297 8100.

Peat Marwick Minato, 17F Hibiya Kokusai Bldg, 2-2-3 Uchisaiwaicho, Chiyoda-ku, Tokyo 100. Tel: (03) 3591 1354.

Rayden Ltd., 4F Shokin Bldg, 8-11-12 Ginza, Chuo-ku, Tokyo 104. Tel: (03) 3571 8023.

SRI East Asia, 9F Imperial Tower, 1-1-1 Uchisaiwaicho, Chiyoda-ku, Tokyo 100. Tel: (03) 3501 7161.

Yano Research Institute, 2-10-1 Nihonbashi Hamacho, Chuo-ku, Tokyo 103. Tel: (03) 3667 0251.

DEPARTMENT STORES EMPLOYING FOREIGNERS IN JAPAN

Hankyu Department Store, 8-7 Kabuta-cho, Kita-ku, Osaka 530. Tel: (06) 361 1381.

Isetan Department Store, 3-14-1 Shinjuku, Shinjuku-ku, Tokyo 160. Tel: (03) 3352 1111.

Mitsukoshi Department Stores, 1-4-1 Nihonbashi Muromachi, Chuo-ku, Tokyo 103. Tel: (03) 3225 2464.

Seibu Department Stores, Sunshine City, 3-1-1 Higashi-Ikebukuro, Toshima-ku, Tokyo 170. Tel: (03) 3989 0111.

Tokyo Group, 1-21-12 Kami-Meguro, Meguro-ku, Tokyo 153. Tel: (03) 3791 6521.

PRINCIPAL ENGLISH LANGUAGE SCHOOLS

AEON, 7F Seiwa Bldg, 2-3-4 Minami Aoyama, Minoat-ku, Tokyo 107. Tel: (03) 3423 4040.

Athenee Francais, 2-11 Suragadai, Kanda, Chiyoda-ku, Tokyo 101. Tel: (03) 3291 3391.

Berlitz School of Language, 7F Yurakucho Bldg, 10-1-1 Yurakucho, Chiyoda-ku, Tokyo 100. Tel: (03) 3214 2611.

Cambridge English School, Nishi-Shinjuku Showa Bldg, 1-13-12, Nishi-Shinjuku, Shinjuku-ku, Tokyo 160. Tel: (03) 3348 0181.

ECC, Dairoku Ara Bldg, 1-5-4 Kabukicho, Shinjuku-ku, Tokyo 160. Tel: (03) 3209 3733.

ELEC, 3-8 Jimbocho, Kanda, Chiyoda-ku, Tokyo 101. Tel: (03) 3265 8911.

GEOS Language System, Matsuoka Tamuracho Bldg, 5-22-10 Shinbashi, Minato-ku, Tokyo 105. Tel: (03) 3459 9840.

Gregg Gaigo Gakko, 1-14-16 Jiyugaoka, Meguro-ku, Tokyo 152. Tel: (03) 3724 0552.

Interac, 2-10-28 Fujimi-cho, Chiyoda-ku, Tokyo 102.
Tel: (03) 3234 7717.
International Language Centre (ILC), Iwanami Jimbocho Bldg, Jinden,
2-1 Jimbocho, Chiyoda-ku, Tokyo. Tel: (03) 3954 5173.
Kanda Gaigo Gakuin, 2-13-13 Uchikanda, Chiyoda-ku, Tokyo 101.
Tel: (03) 3254 2731.
Nichibei Kaiwa Gakko, 1-21 Yosuya, Shinjuku-ku, Tokyo 160.
Tel: (03) 3359 9621.
Sony Eigo Kyoshitsu, Kurihara Bldg, 1-6-12 Nishi-Shimbashi, Minato-
ku, Tokyo. Tel: (03) 3232 0290.
Time Communications Ltd., Time & Life Bldg, 3-6 Otemachi 2-chome,
Chiyoda-ku, Tokyo 100. Tel: (03) 3270 4711.
Tokyo Business Gaigo Senmon Gakko, 1-14-6 Jiyugaoka, Meguro-ku,
Tokyo 152. Tel: (03) 3724 0551.
Tokyo Foreign Language College, 7-3-8 Nishi-Shinjuku, Shinjuku-ku,
Tokyo 160. Tel: (03) 3367 1101.

INTERNATIONAL SCHOOLS EMPLOYING FOREIGNERS IN JAPAN

American School in Japan, 1-1 Nomizu 1-chome, Chofu-shi, Tokyo 182.
Tel: (0422) 31 6351.
The British School in Tokyo, 1-21-18 Shibuya, Shibuya-ku, Tokyo 150.
Tel: (03) 3400 7353.
Canandian Academy, 3-1 Nagaminedai 2-chome, Nada-ku, Kobe.
Tel: (078) 881 5211.
Christian Academy in Japan, Shinkawa-cho 1-chome, Higashi Kurume-
shi, Tokyo 203. Tel: (0424) 71 0022.
Fukuoka International School, 1-28 Maedashi 4-chome, Higashi-ku,
Fukuoka-shi 813. Tel: (092) 641 0326.
Hiroshima International School, 2-6 Ushita-Naka 2-chome, Hiroshima
730. Tel: (082) 221 622.
Hokkaido International School, 41-8 Fukuzami, Toyohira-ku, Sapporo,
Hokkaido 062. Tel: (011) 851 1205.
International School of the Sacred Heart, 3-1 Hiroo 4-chome, Shibuya-
ku, Tokyo 150. Tel: (03) 34 3951.
Kyoto International School, Ichijodori, Muromachi Nishi-Iru, Kamikyo-
ku, Kyoto 602.
Marist Brothers International School, 2-1 Chimori-cho 1-chome, Suma-
ku, Kobe 654. Tel: (078) 732 6266.
Nagoya International School, 2686 Minamihara, Nakashidami,
Moriyama-ku, Nagoya 463.

Nishimachi International School, 14-7 Moto-Azabu 2-chome, Minato-ku, Tokyo 106. Tel: (03) 3451 5520.

Okinawa Christian School, PO Box 42, Urasoshi, Okinawa 901-22. Tel: (0988) 77 3661.

Sendai American School, 1-28 Tsuchitoi 1-chome, Sendai 980.

St. Mary's International School for Boys, 6-19 Seta 1-chome, Setagaya-ku, Tokyo 158. Tel: (03) 3709 3411.

St. Maur International School, 83 Bluff, maka-ku, Yokohama 231. Tel: (045) 641 5751.

Santa Maria International School, 2-2-4 Minami Tanaka, Nerima-ku, Tokyo 77. Tel: (03) 3904 0509.

St. Michael's International School, 5 Naka Yamatedori 3-chome, Ikuta-ku, Kobe 650. Tel: (078) 231 8885.

Yokohama International School, 2-5-8 Yamate-cho, Maka-ku, Yokohama 231. Tel: (045) 622 0084.

JAPANESE UNIVERSITIES EMPLOYING FOREIGNERS IN JAPAN

Asia University, 5-24-10 Sakae, Musashino-shi, Tokyo 180. Tel: (0422) 54 3111.

Bunka Women's University, Yoyogi 3-22-1, Shibuya-ku, Tokyo 151. Tel: (03) 3299 2311.

Chiba University, 1-33 Yayoi-cho, Chiba-shi, Chiba-ken 260. Tel: (0472) 51 1111.

Chuo University, 742-1 Higashi-Nakano, Hachioji-shi, Tokyo 192-03. Tel: (0426) 74 2212.

Doshisha University, Karasuma Higashi, Imedagawa Doori, Kamigyo-ku, Kyoto-shi, Kyoto-fu 602. Tel: (075) 251 3260.

Hiroshima University, 1-1-89 Higashi Senda-cho, Naka-ku, Hiroshima-shi, Hiroshima-ken 730. Tel: (082) 241 1221.

Hokkaido University, Kita 8 Nishi 5, Kita-ku, Sapporo-shi, Hokkaido 060. Tel: (011) 716 2111.

Hosei University, 2-17-1 Fujimi, Chiyoda-ku, Tokyo 102. Tel: (03) 3264 9662.

Kansai University, 3-3-35 Yamate-cho, Suita-shi, Osaka 564. Tel: (06) 388 1121.

Kinki University, 3-4-1 Kowakoe, Osaka-shi, Higashi, Osaka 577. Tel: (06) 721 2332.

Kobe University. 1-1 kokkodai-cho, Nada-ku, Kobe-shi, Hyog-ken 657. Tel: (078) 881 1212.

Komazawa University, 1-23-1 Komazawa, Setagaya-ku, Tokyo 154.
Tel: (03) 3418 9562.
Kyoto University, Yoshida Homachi, Sakyo-ku, Kyoto-shi, Kyoto-fu 606.
Tel: (075) 753 7531.
Kyushu University, 6-10-1 Hakozaki, Hagashi-ku, Fukuoka-shi,
Fukuoka-ken 812. Tel: (092) 641 1101.
Meiji University, Kanda Surugadai 1-1, Chiyoda-ku, Tokyo 101.
Tel: (03) 3296 4144.
Nagoya University, Furo-cho, Chikusa-ku, Nagoya-shi, Aichi-ken 464.
Tel: (052) 781 5111.
Niho University, 4-8-24 Kudan Minami, Chiyoda-ku, Tokyo 102.
Tel: (03) 3236 2271.
Okayama University, 1-1-1 Tsushimanaka, Okayama-shi, Okayama-ken
700. Tel: (0862) 52 1111.
Osaka University, 1-1 Yamadaoka, Suita-shi, Osaka-fu 565.
Tel: (06) 877 5111.
Rikkyo University, 3-34-1 Nishi Ikebukuro, Toshima-ku, Tokyo 171.
Tel: (03) 3985 2208.
Ritsumeikan University, Kitamachi, Tojii, Kita-ku, Kyoto-shi, Kyoto-fu
603. Tel: (075) 465 1111.
Saitama University, 255 Shimo Okubo, Urawa-shi, Saitama-ken 338.
Tel: (048) 852 2111.
Sophia University, 7-1 Kioi-cho, Chiyoda-ku, Tokyo 102.
Tel: (03) 3288 3111.
Tenri University, Samanouchi-cho, Tenri-shi, Nara-shi 632.
Tel: (0743) 63 1511.
Tohoku University, 2-1-1 Kathira, Sendai-shi, Miyagi-ken 9480.
Tel: (022) 227 6200.
Tokyo International University, 1-13-1 Matoba-kita, Kawagoe-shi,
Saitama-shi, Saitama-ken 350. Tel: (0492) 32 1111.
Tokyo University, 5-28-20 Hakusan, Bunkyo-ku, Tokyo 112.
Tel: (03) 3945 7557.
University of Osaka Prefecture, 4-8-4 Mozo Umemachi, Sakai-shi,
Osaka-fu 591. Tel: (0722) 52 1161.
University of Tsukuba, 1-1-1 Tennodai, Tsukuba-shi, Ibaragi-ken 305.
Tel: (2948) 53 2111.
Waseda University, 1-6-1 Nishi Waseda, Shinjuku-ku, Tokyo 169.
Tel: (03) 3203 4141.
Yokohama National University, Tokiwadai, Hodogaya-ku, Yokohama-
shi, Kanagawa-ken 156. Tel: (045) 335 1451.

LAW FIRMS EMPLOYING FOREIGNERS IN JAPAN

Adachi, Henderson, Miyatake & Fujita, 1001 Time Life Bldg, 2-3-6 Otemachi, Otemachi, Tokyo. Tel: (03) 3270 7461.

Allen & Overy, 5F NSE Bldg, 1-7-1 Kanda Jinbocho, Chiyoda-ku, Tokyo 101. Tel: (03) 3259 9898.

Amida, Hirokawa & Doi, 306 Ohe Bldg, 2-8-1 Nishi Tenma, Kita-ku, Osaka 530. Tel: (06) 361 9095.

Anderson, Mori & Rabonowitz, 6F AIU Bldg, 1-1-3 Marunouchi, Chiyoda-ku, Tokyo 100. Tel: (03) 3214 1371.

Aoki, Christensen & Nomoto, 720 New Tokyo Bldg, 3-3-1 Marunouchi, Chiyoda-ku, Tokyo 100. Tel: (03) 3211 8871.

Blakemore & Mitsuki, 912 Iino Bldg, 2-2-1 Uchisaiwai-cho, Chiyoda-ku, Tokyo 100. Tel: (03) 3503 5571.

Braun, Moriya, Hoashi & Kubota, 911 Iino Bldg, 2-2-1 Uchisaiwai-cho, Chiyoda-ku, Tokyo 100. Tel: (03) 3504 0251.

Clifford Chance, 6F South Hill Nagatocho Bldg, 1-11-30 Nagatacho, Chiyoda-ku, Tokyo 100. Tel: (03) 3581 4311.

Denton, Hall, Burgin & Warrens, 2F Ichibancho 27 Bldg, 27 Ichibancho, Chiyoda-ku, Tokyo 102. Tel: (03) 3222 5977.

Freshfields, 8F Ark Mori Bldg, 1-12-32 Akasaka, Minato-ku, Tokyo 107. Tel: (03) 3583 3483.

Furness, Sato & Ishizawa, 17F Fukoku Seimei Bldg, 2-2-2 Uchisaiwai-cho, Chiyoda-ku, Tokyo 100. Tel: (03) 3508 0721.

Linklaters & Paines, 3F Mitsui Kyowa Bldg, 1-1 Kanada Suda-cho, Chiyoda-ku, Tokyo 101. Tel: (03) 3258 3691.

Logan, Okamoto & Takashima, 330 New Otemachi Bldg, 2-2-1 Otemachi, Chiyoda-ku, Tokyo 100. Tel: (03) 3242 6181.

Lovell White Durrant, 20F Shin-Kasumigaseki Bldg, 3-3-2 Kasumigaseki, Chiyoda-ku, Tokyo 100. Tel: (03) 3503 0699.

McKenna & Co., 4F AIOS Gotanada Annex, 1-7-11 Higashi-Gotanda, Shinagawa-ku, Tokyo 141. Tel: (03) 3440 8546.

Midosuji Law Office Toyoda Bldg, 4-3-11 Minami Senba, Minami-ku, Osaka 542. Tel: (06) 251 7266.

Mori Sogo Law Office, 5F Dpwa Bldg, 3-11-3 Akasaka, Minato-ku, Tokyo 107. Tel: (03) 35722 6641.

Nagashima & Ono, 4-9-22 Akasaka, Minato-ku, Tokyo 107. Tel: (03) 3404 9171.

Nakagawa Godo Law Office, Aasaka Nakagawa Bldg, 3-11-3 Akasaka, Minato-ku, Tokyo 107. Tel: (03) 3589 2921.

Nishimura & Sanada, 4F Kasumigaseki Bldg, 2-5 Kasumigaseki 2-chome, Chiyoda-ku, Tokyo 100. Tel: (03) 3593 3912.

Oh & Ebashi, 803 Umeda Dashinmichi Bldg, 1-1-5 Dojima, Kita-ku, Osaka 530. Tel: (06) 341 0461.

Ohara & Kano, 903 City Coop, 2-2-7 Minami Morimachi, Kita-ku, Osaka 530. Tel: (06) 313 1208.

Richards Butler, Sunbridge Ogawamachi Bldg, 2-2 Kanda Ogawamachi, Chiyoda-ku, Tokyo 101. Tel: (03) 3292 2500.

Tokyo Aoyama Law Office, 410 Aoyama Bldg, 1-2-3 Kita Aoyama, Minato-ku, Tokyo 107. Tel: (03) 3403 5281.

Tsuchiya, Sakuragi, Sogo & Ito, 925 Hibiya Park Bldg, 1-8-1 Yurakucho, Chiyoda-ku, Tokyo 100. Tel: (03) 3201 0401.

MEDIA COMPANIES EMPLOYING FOREIGNERS IN JAPAN

Newspapers and wire services

Asahi Evening News, 8-5 Tsukiji 7-chome, Chuo-ku, Tokyo 104. Tel: (03) 3546 7132.

Daily Yomiuri, 1-7-1 Ohtemachi, Chiyoda-ku, Tokyo 100-55. Tel: (03) 3242 1111.

Far Eastern Economic Review, 1-9-5 Otemachi, Chiyoda-ku, Tokyo 100. Tel: (03) 3241 2920.

Japan Times, 4-5-4 Shibaura, Minato-ku, Tokyo 108. Tel: (03) 3452 1799.

Mainichi Daily News, Hitotsubashi 1-1-1, Chiyoda-ku, Tokyo 100-51. Tel: (03) 3212 0321.

Agence France Presses, Asahi Shibun Bldg, 5-3-2 Tsukiji, Chuo-ku, Tokyo 104. Tel: (03) 3545 3061.

Associated Press, 11F Asahi Shinbun Bldg, 5-3-2 Tsukiji, Chuo-ku, Tokyo 104. Tel: (03) 3545 5901.

Knight Ridder Financial News, Ichibancho F.S. Bldg, 8 Ichibancho, Chiyoda-ku, Tokyo 102. Tel: (03) 3230 1155.

Kyodo News Service, 2-2-5 Toranomon, Minato-ku, Tokyo 105. Tel: (03) 3505 6630.

Nikkei International, 1-4-13 Uchikanda, Chiyoda-ku, Tokyo 101. Tel: (03) 3293 2796.

Reuters Japan, Shuwa Kamiyacho Bldg, 4-3-13 Toranomon, Minato-ku, Tokyo 105. Tel: (03) 3505 6630.

United Press International, Palaceside Bldg, 1-1-1 Hitotsubashi, Chiyoda-ku, Tokyo 100. Tel: (03) 3121 7911.

The Wall Street Journal/The Asian Wall Street Journal, Nihon Keizai Shinbun Bldg, 1-9-5 Ohtemachi, Chiyoda-ku, Tokyo 100. Tel: (03) 3246 1098.

Magazines

Business Tokyo, Keizaikai Bldg, 2-13-18 Minami-Aoyama, Minato-ku, Tokyo 107. Tel: (03) 3423 8500.

Far East Traveller, 1-4-28 Moto-Azabu, Minato-ku, Tokyo 106. Tel:(03) 3452 0474.

Look Japan, 2-2 Kanda Ogawa-machi, Chiyoda-ku, Tokyo 101. Tel:(03) 3291 8955.

The Tokyo Journal, Cross-Cultural Communications Bldg, 12-2-1 Minami Motomachi, Shinjuku-ku, Tokyo 160. Tel: (03) 5379 6219.

Tokyo Weekender, Oriental Bldg, 1-55-11 Nakano-ku, Tokyo 164. Tel: (03) 3374 2631.

TV and radio

BBC, Nihon Terebi, 4-Bancho, 5-6 Chiyoda-ku, Tokyo. Tel: (03) 3288 0010.

KYTO International Radio, 7F Togensha Bldg, 1-19 Sumiyoshi-cho, Shinjuku-ku, Tokyo 162. Tel: (03) 3359 5100.

NHK, NHK Hoso Center, 2-2-1 Jinnan, Shibuya-ku, Tokyo. Tel: (03) 3465 1111.

Tokyo FM Broadcasting, 1-7 Kojimachi, Chiyoda-ku, Tokyo 107. Tel: (03) 3584 3111.

Visnews, Aoki Bldg, 4-1-10 Toranomon, Minato-ku, Tokyo 105. Tel: (03) 3433 8351.

Publishing

Addison-Wesley Publishers (Japan) Ltd., Nichibo Bldg, 1-2-2 Sakuracho, Chiyoda-ku, Tokyo. Tel: (03) 3291 4581.

Charles E. Tuttle Co., Suido 1-chome, 26 Bunkyo-ku, Tokyo 112. Tel: (03) 3811 7106.

Harcourt Brace Jovanovich Japan Inc., Ichibancho Central Bldg, 22-1 Ichibancho, Chiyoda-ku, Tokyo 102. Tel: (03) 3234 3913.

Kodansha International Ltd., 17-14 Otowa 1-chome, Bunkyo-ku, Tokyo 112. Tel: (03) 3944 6493.

Longman Penguin Japan, Yamaguchi Bldg, 2-12-9 Kanda Jinbocho, Chiyoda-ku, Tokyo 101. Tel: (03) 3265 7627.

McGraw Hill, Room 1528, Kasumigaseki Bldg, 3-2-5 Kasumigaseki, Chiyoda-ku, Tokyo 100. Tel: (03) 3581 9816.

Weatherhill, 7-6-12 Roppongi, Minato-ku, Tokyo 106. Tel: (03) 3263 4391.

PRINCIPAL MODELLING AGENCIES DEALING WITH FOREIGNERS IN JAPAN

Askew Japan, 3-10-7 Minami Aoyama, Minato-ku, Tokyo 107.
Tel: (03) 3478 1232.
Shinseifu Bldg, 1-2-19 Nakatsu, Oyodo-ku, Osaka
Tel: (06) 373 1524.
Boa Agency, 2-1-1021 Udagawacho, Shibuya-ku, Tokyo.
Tel: (03) 3476 1516.
Central Fashion, Aoyama Tower Bldg, 2-24-15 Minami Aoyama,
Minato-ku, Tokyo 107. Tel: (03) 3405 9111.
Fame Promotion Inc., 326 Gaien House, 2-2-39 Jingumae, Shibuya-ku,
Tokyo. Tel: (03) 478 5541.
Folio Inc., 3-4-8 Azabudai, Minato-ku, Tokyo 106.
Tel: (03) 3586 6481.
Japan Fashion Model Center, 5-10-14 Minami Aoyama, Minato-ku,
Tokyo 107. Tel: (03) 3400 9571.
Japan Model International Co., 3-5-3-405 Nishi-Shinjuku, Tokyo 106.
Tel: (03) 3478 7671.
K & M Promotions, 2-10-25 Kita Aoyama, Minato-ku, Tokyo.
Tel: (03) 3404 9429.
Mademoiselle Model Group, 1-10-10 Nishi Ebisu, Shibuya-ku, Tokyo
150. Tel: (03) 3464 7901.
Society of Style, 8-12-13 Ginza, Chuo-ku, Tokyo 104.
Tel: (03) 3542 7901.

MUSIC VENUES KNOWN TO HIRE FOREIGN ARTISTS

Body & Soul, Roppongi, Tokyo. Tel: (03) 3408 2094.
The Carnival, Kabuki-cho, Shinjuku, Tokyo. Tel: (03) 3200 1261.
Inaoiza, Koenji, Tokyo. Tel: (03) 3336 4480.
La Petit Rue, Harajuku, Tokyo. Tel: (03) 3400 9890.
Someday, Shin Okubo, Tokyo. Tel: (03) 3207 1818.
Club Z, Koenji, Tokyo. Tel: (03) 3336 5841.

TRADING COMPANIES EMPLOYING FOREIGNERS IN JAPAN

C. Itoh & Co. Ltd., 1 Kita-Aoyama 2-chrome, Minato-ku, Tokyo 107-
77. Tel: (03) 3497 2983.
Kawasaki Enterprises Inc., Shuwa Shiba Park Bldg, 2-4-1 Shibakoen,
Minato-ku, Tokyo 105. Tel: (03) 3578 6012.
Mitsui & Co., 1-2-1 Otemachi, Chiyoda-ku, Tokyo 100.
Tel: (03) 3285 1111.

Mitsubishi Trading Co., 2-6-3 Marunouchi, Chiyoda-ku, Tokyo 100. Tel: (03) 3210 2121.

Marubeni Corporation, 4-2 Ohtemachi 1-chome, Chiyoda-ku, Tokyo 100-88. Tel: (03) 3282 7096.

Nichimen Corporation, PO Box Central 1136, 11-1 Nihonbashi 3-chome, Chuo-ku, Tokyo 103. Tel: (03) 3277 5564.

Nissho Iwai Corporation, 4-5 Akasaka 2-chrome, Minato-ku, Tokyo 107. Tel: (03) 3588 4038.

Orix Corporation, 35F World Trade Center Bldg, 2-4-1 Hamamatsu-cho, Minato-ku, Tokyo 105. Tel: (03) 3435 6782.

Sumitomo Shoji, 2-2 Hitotsubashi 1-chrome, Chiyoda-ku, Tokyo 100. Tel: (03) 3217 5000.

TRANSLATING COMPANIES EMPLOYING FOREIGNERS IN JAPAN

Investor Relations Japan, 1-15-13 Yotsuya, Shinjuku-ku, Tokyo 160. Tel: (03) 3351 1120.

Japan Convention Services, Nippon Press Center Bldg, 2-2-1 Uchisaiwaicho, Chiyoda-ku, Tokyo 100. Tel: (03) 3508 1211.

Japan Interpreters Association, Chiyoda Seimei Bldg, 1-5-20 Takadanobaba, Shinjuku-ku, Tokyo. Tel: (03) 3209 4741.

Japan Translation Center, 1-21 kanda, Nishikicho, Chiyoda-ku, Tokyo 101. Tel: (03) 3291 0655.

Kokusai Enterprises, 1-2-1 Minami Naruse, Machida-shi, Tokyo 104. Tel: (0427) 23 8221.

Simul International Inc., Kowa Bldg, no. 9, 8-10 Akasaka 1-chrome, Minato-ku, Tokyo 107. Tel: (03) 3586 5641.

UK COMPANIES WITH BRANCHES/SUBSIDIARIES IN JAPAN

ACI Japan Ltd., Yurakucho Bldg, 1-10-1 Yurakucho, Chiyoda-ku, Tokyo 100. Tel: (03) 3213 2561. (Part of the BTR group. Manufacters of industrial adhesives)

Alfred Dunhill, 8F Kokusai Bldg, 2-13-11 Kayabachho, Nihonbashi, Chuo-ku, Tokyo 103. Tel: (03) 3667 6731. (Markets Dunhill products in Japan).

Allen & Overy, 5F NSE Bldg, 1-7-1 Kanada Jimbo-cho, Chiyoda-ku, Tokyo 101. Tel: (03) 3259 9898. (Leading international law firm).

APV, No 2 Katsuya Bldg, 23-23 Sakuragaoka-cho, Shibuya-ku, Tokyo 150. Tel: (03) 3463 9161. (Produces processing machinery for the food industry).

Baring Securities (Japan) Ltd, 10F Shin Kasumigaseki Bldg, 3-3-2

Kasumigaseki, Chiyoda-ku, Tokyo 100. Tel: (03) 3595 8811. (Stock broker).

BOC Japan, Ando Fukuyoshi Bldg, 1-11-28 Akasaka, Minato-ku, Tokyo 107. Tel: (03) 3589 2451. (Industrial gases and health care).

British Aerospace, 9F Toho Bldg, 2-5-1 Akasaka, Minato-ku, Tokyo 107. Tel: (03) 3587 0052.

The British Council Cambridge English School, 1-2 Kagurazaka, Shinjuku-ku, Tokyo 162. Tel: (03) 3235 8011.

The British Insurance Group, Tokyo Kokusai Bldg, 3-1-1 Marunouchi, Chiyoda-ku, Tokyo 100. Tel: (03) 3214 6921.

BP Far East, Kasumigaseki Bldg, 3-2-5 Kasumigaseki, Chiyoda-ku, Tokyo 100. Tel: (03) 3592 3928.

The British School in Tokyo, 1-21-18 Shibuya, Shibuya-ku, Tokyo 150. Tel: (03) 3400 7353. (Co-educational primary school).

British Technology Group, Rayden (Japan) Ltd., 4F Shokin Bldg, 8-11-12 Ginza, Chuo-ku, Tokyo 104. (Technology transferand licensing).

British Telecom, 33F Ark Mori Bldg, 1-12-32 Akasaka, Minato-ku, Tokyo 107. Tel: (03) 3505 5858.

British Tourist Authority, 246 Tokyo Club Bldg, 3-2-6 Kasumigaseki, Chiyoda-ku, Tokyo 100. Tel: (03) 3581 3603.

Burrups Japan Ltd., Ishihara Bldg, 3-3-12 Iidabashi, Chiyoda-ku, Tokyo 102. Tel: (03) 3238 0621. (Subsidiary of St. Ives PLC., UK's largest printer).

Cable & Wireless (Japan) Ltd., 7F Bridgestone Toranomom Bldg, 3-25-2 Toranomon, Minato-ku, Tokyo 105. Tel: (03) 3470 2100. (Telecommunications).

Casters Japan Inc., 3F Ematanaka Bldg, 3-5-2 Iidabashi, Chiyoda-ku, Tokyo 102. Tel: (03) 3238 0341. (International Executive Search Agency).

Castrol K.K., Izumiya Bldg, 1-3 Kojimachi, Chiyoda-ku, Tokyo 102. Tel: (03) 3265 6101.

Chestertons International Property Consultants, Madre Matsuda Bldg, 4-13 Kioi-cho, Chiyoda-ku, Tokyo 102. Tel: (03) 3234 1101.

Chuo Coopers & Lybrand, Box 50, Kasumigaseki Bldg, Tokyo 100. Tel: (03) 3592 2821.

Clifford Chance, 6F South Hill Nagatacho Bldg, 1-11-30 Nagatacho, Chiyoda-ku, Tokyo 100. Tel: (03) 3581 4311.

Coats Viyella PLC., Japan Representative Office, ABS Bldg, 2-4-16 Kudan Minami, Chiyoda-ku, Tokyo 102. Tel: (03) 3239 2817. (Coats Viyella is one of the world's largest textile manufacturers).

Commercial Union Assurance Company/Commercial Union Asset

Management (Japan), 10F Kioicho Bldg, 3-12 Kioicho, Chiyoda-ku, Tokyo 102. Tel: (03) 3238 2638.

Cornes & Co. Ltd., 8F Maruzen Bldg, 2-3-10 Nihonbashi, Chuo-ku, Tokyo 103. Tel: (03) 3272 5771. (Represents UK companies in Japan).

Courtaulds Japan Ltd., DF Bldg, 2-2-8 Aoyama, Minato-ku, Tokyo 107. Tel: (03) 3479 3771.

Currie & Brown, Gosei Bldg, 5-16-7 Minami Azabu, Minato-ku, Tokyo 106. Tel: (03) 3442 6642. (Building and civil engineering).

Danzas K.K., 8F Toyo Bldg, 2-2-22 Mita, Minato-ku, Tokyo 108. Tel: (03) 3769 5598. (Cargo specialist).

Davy Corp, PLC., Shokin Bldg, 8-11-12 Ginza, Chuo-ku, Tokyo 104. Tel: (03) 3571 2297. (Engineering and construction).

Denton, Hall, Burgin & Warrens, 2F Ichibancho 27 Bldg, 27 Ichibancho, Chiyoda-ku, Tokyo 102. Tel: (03) 3222 5977. (International law firm).

Dewe Rogerson, 5F Watase Bldg, 3-5-0 Nishi-Shinbashi, Minato-ku, Tokyo 105. Tel: (03) 3438 1781. (Corporate communciations specialists).

Eastman Chemicals (Japan) Ltd., Gotenmaya Mori Bldg, 4-7-35 Kita-Shinagawa, Shinagawa-ku, Tokyo 140. Tel: (03) 5488 2100. (Chemicals suppliers).

The Financial Times, Kasahara Bldg, 1-6-10 Uchikanda, Chiyoda-ku, Tokyo 101. Tel: (03) 3295 1990.

Fisons Pharamceuticals, (Liaison Office), 7F Kawaramachi Bldg, 4-2-14 Kawaramachi, Chuo-ku, Osaka 541. Tel: (06) 232 3933.

Freshfields, 8F Ark Mori Bldg, 1-12-32 Akasaka, Minato-ku, Tokyo 107. Tel: (03) 3583 3483.

Gallaher International, Prestige Products Promotions Inc., 3-12 Kanda Nishikicho, Chiyoda-ku, Tokyo 101. Tel: (03) 3290 2572.

GKR Japan Ltd., 8F Landmark Shibakoen Bldg, 1-2-6 Shiba-koen, Minato-ku, Tokyo 105. Tel: (03) 3578 9686. (International executive search agency).

Gillespies, 5F Nichimen Bldg, 1-13-1 Kyobashi, Chuo-ku, Tokyo 104. Tel: (03) 3277 8759. (Enviroment and landscape design).

Hambros Bank Ltd., 5F Fukoku Seimei Bldg, 2-2-2 Uchisaiwai-cho, Chiyoda-ku, Tokyo 100. Tel: (03) 3508 2141.

HHL (Japan) Ltd., No. 31 Kowa Bldg, 3-19-1 Shiroganedai, Minato-ku, Tokyo 108. Tel: (03) 3449 5522. (Insurance brokers).

Hill Samuel, Tokyo Representative Office, 6F Tokyo Shoyu Kaikan Bldg, 3-3-1 Kasumigaseki, Chiyoda-ku, Tokyo 100. Tel: (03) 35016491.

ICI Japan Ltd., Palace Bldg, 1-1-1 Marunouchi, Chiyoda-ku, Tokyo. Tel: (03) 3211 6661.

Inchape Dodwell & Co., Togin Bldg, 1-4-2 Marunouchi, Chiyoda-ku, Tokyo 102. Tel: (03) 3211 2140.

ICL Ltd., 4-9-1 Shibaura, Minato-ku, Tokyo 108. Tel: (03) 3798 4726.

International Textiles Inc., 5F D.F. Bldg, 2-2-8 Minami Aoyama, Minato-ku, Tokyo 107. Tel: (03) 3479 3311.

Jaguar Japan, 3-7-2 Oyamadai, Setagaya-ku, Tokyo 158. Tel: (03) 3702 7211.

James Chapel Pacific, 7F Kokusai Bldg, 3-1-1 Marunouchi, Chiyoda-ku, Tokyo 100. Tel: (03) 3282 0111.

Jardine Matheson K.K., Nisseki Honkan, 1-3-12 Nishi-Shimbashi, Minato-ku, Tokyo 105. Tel: (03) 3502 1421. (Trading company).

Jardine Wines & Spirits, Halifax Onarimon Bldg, 3-24-10 Nishi-Shinbashi, Minato-ku, Tokyo 105. Tel: (03) 3434 1825.

John Swire & Sons (Japan) Ltd., Swire House, 14 Ichibancho, Chiyoda-ku, Tokyo 102. Tel: (03) 3230 9300.

Jones, Lang, Wootton K.K., 1001 Marunouchi Mitsui Bldg, 2-2-2 Marunouchi, Chiyoda-ku, Tokyo 100. Tel: (03) 3216 3631. (International real estate consultancy).

Kleinwort Benson International Inc., 810 Kokusai Bldg, 3-1-1 Marunouchi, Chiyoda-ku, Tokyo 100. Tel: (03) 3218 0800.

Knight, Frank & Rutley, 7F Shirai Bldg, 5-12-13 Toranomon, Minato-ku, Tokyo 105. Tel: (03) 3578 9071. (Property business).

Laura Ashley Japan Ltd., Honey Bldg, Aoyama, 3-35-8 Jingumae, Shibuya-ku, Tokyo 150. Tel: (03) 5474 2641.

Linklaters & Paines, 3F Mitsui Kyowa Bldg, 1-1 Kanda Suda-cho, Chiyoda-ku, Tokyo 101. Tel: (03) 3258 3691.

Lloyds Bank PLC., Ote Center Bldg, 1-1-3 Ohtemachi, Chiyoda-ku, Tokyo. Tel: (03) 3214 6771.

Lloyd's Register of Shipping, No. 32 Mori Bldg, 3-4-30 Shiba Koen, Minato-ku, Tokyo 105. Tel: (03) 3438 0481.

Lovell White Durrant, 20F Shi-Kasumigaseki Bldg, 3-3-2 Kasumigaseki, Chiyoda-ku, Tokyo 100. Tel: (03) 3503 0699. (International law firm).

McKenna & Co., 4F AIOS Gotanda Annex, 1-7-11 Higashi-Gotanda, Shinagawa-ku, Tokyo 141. Tel: (03) 3440 8546. (International law firm).

Metcalfe Cooper Ltd., 103 Hills Magome, Ota-ku, Tokyo, Japan. Tel: (03) 3775 9718. (Producer/distributor of corporate literature).

Midland Bank PLC., AIU Bldg, 1-1-3 Marunouchi, Chiyoda-ku, Tokyo 100. Tel: (03) 3284 1861.

N.M. Rothschild & Sons, 14F AIU Bldg, 1-1-3 Marunouchi, Chiyoda-ku, Tokyo 100. Tel: (03) 3201 8601.

National Westminster Bank PLC, AIU Bldg, 1-1-3 Marunouchi, Chiyoda-ku, Tokyo 100. Tel: (03) 3216 5301.

P & O Containers, Swire House, 14 Ichibancho, Chiyoda-ku, Tokyo 102. Tel: (03) 3230 9110.

Price Waterhouse, Aoyama Bldg, 1-2-3 Kita-Aoyama, Minato-ku, Tokyo 107. Tel: (03) 3404 9351.

Quantel K.K., TBR Bldg, 5-7 Kojimachi Bldg, Chiyoda-ku, Tokyo 102. Tel: (03) 3221 0761. (Sales and marketing of own range graphics products).

Richards Butler, Sunbridge, Ogawamachi Bldg, 2-2 Kanda Ogawamachi, Chiyoda-ku, Tokyo 101. Tel: (03) 3292 2500. (International law firm).

Rio Tinto-Zinc (Japan), 502 Kokusai Bldg, 3-1-1 Marunouchi, Chiyoda-ku, Tokyo 100. Tel: (03) 3212 3841.

Rover Japan Ltd., 3-16-18 Shibaura, Minato-ku, Tokyo 108. Tel: (03) 33457 0871.

Royal Bank of Scotland PLC., Dai-Ichi Seimei Sogo Kan, 3-7-1 Kyobashi, Chuo-ku, Tokyo 104. Tel: (03) 3567 7078.

Royal Doulton Dodwell K.K., 2F No. 35 Kowa Bldg, 1-14-14 Akasaka, Minato-ku, Tokyo 107. Tel: (03) 3589 2661.

S.G. Warburg Securities (Japan) Inc., New Edobashi Bldg, 1-7-2 Nihonbashi Honcho, Chuo-ku, Tokyo 103. Tel: (03) 3246 4111.

Schroders Securities (Japan) Ltd., 26F Ark Mori Bldg, 1-12-32 Akasaka, Minato-ku, Tokyo 107. Tel: (03) 5562 8800.

Sedgewick James Far East, 3F No. 16 Kowa Bldg, 1-9-20 Akasaka, Minato-ku, Tokyo 107. Tel: (03) 3582 2321. (Insurance).

Shell Kagaku K.K., Kasumigaseki Bldg, 3-2-5 Kasumigaseki, Chiyoda-ku, Tokyo 100. Tel: (03) 3581 6597.

Smith Kline Beecham Seiyaku K.K., 6 Sanbancho, Chiyoda-ku, Tokyo 102. Tel: (03) 3221 5811.

Standard Chartered Bank, Fuji Bldg, 3-2-3 Maruouchi, Chiyoda-ku, Tokyo 100. Tel: (03) 3213 6541.

Thorn EMI PLC., 8F Kiocho Bldg, Chiyoda-ku, Tokyo 102. Tel: (03) 3237 5855.

TI Group, ABS Bldg, 2-4-16 Kudan-Minami, Chiyoda-ku, Tokyo 102. Tel: (03) 3221 9785. (Engineering).

United Distillers Japan Ltd., Sumitomo Gtanda Bldg, 7-1-1 Nishi-Gotanda, Shinagawa-ku, Tokyo. Tel: (03) 3491 3011.

Varity (Japan) K.K., 5F Reinanzaka Bldg, 1-14-2 Akasaka, Minato-ku, Tokyo 107. Tel: (03) 3586 7377.

Vickers Japan, 2F Maekawa Bldg, 2-3-7 Kudan-Kita, Chiyoda-ku, Tokyo
102. Tel: (03) 3237 6861.

Willett K.K., 3-21-3 Nishi Azabu, Minato-ku, Tokyo 106.
Tel: (03) 3403 5631.

PROFESSIONAL ORGANISATIONS

Advertising

International Advertising Association, Kochiwa Bldg, 4-8-12 Ginza,
Chuo-ku, Tokyo. Tel: (03) 3561 6353.

Architecture/construction/engineering

Far East Society of Architects & Engineers, Nippon Construction, 2-34
Ichigaya Tamachi, Shinjuku-ku, Tokyo 162. Tel: (03) 3267 786.

Finance

Securities Public Exchange Information Center, 1-5-8 Kayabacho,
Nihonbashi, Chuo-ku, Tokyo 103. Tel: (03) 3667 2754.

Legal

Japan Lawyer's Association, Kasumigaseki 1-1-1, Chiyoda-ku, Tokyo.
Tel: (03) 3209 4741.

Roppongi Bar Association. Tel: (03) 3280 2847.

Media

Foreign Correspondents Club of Japan, Yurakucho Denki Bldg, 1-7-1
Yurakucho, Chiyoda-ku, Tokyo. Tel: (03) 3211 3161.

Foreign Press Center, Nippon Press Center Bldg, 2-2-1 Uchisaiwai-cho,
Chiyoda-ku, Tokyo. Tel: (03) 3501 3401.

Forum for Corporate Communications. Tel: (03) 3433 3874.

Media Research Center, Irimajiri Bldg, 6-40 Shin Ogawa-cho, Shinjuku-
ku, Tokyo 162. Tel: (03) 3267 6551.

National Association of Commercial Broadcasters, Bungei Shunju Bldg,
3-23 Kioi-cho, Chiyoda-ku, Tokyo 102. Tel: (03) 3265 7481.

Society of Writers, Editors & Translators (SWET), 2-19-15-808 Shibuya,
Shibuya-ku, Tokyo 150.

Japan Association of Translators, 2-31-20-607 Shimo-toda, Toda, Saitama
335. Tel: (0484) 44 85647.

Japan Interpreter's Association, 1-5-20 Takadanobaba, Shinjuku-ku,
Tokyo 169. Tel: (03) 3209 4741.

Society of Technical Communication. Tel: (03) 3455 8711.

Teaching

Japan Association of English Teachers (JALT), 6-26 Hirakata
Motomachi, Hirakata-shi, Osaka 573. Tokyo, Tel: (03) 3444 8474.
Kyoto, Tel: (075) 392 2291.

Association of English Teachers of Children, 2-7-11 Takaido Higashi,
Suginami-ku, Tokyo 168. Tel: (0422) 53 0024.
Association of Foreign Teachers in Japan. Tel: (03) 3238 3909.

Tourism

Foreigners in Travel. Tel: (03) 3454 6339.

NETWORKING AND GENERAL SUPPORT ORGANISATIONS

KAISHA, The Kaisha Society, c/o The Press Club, 20F Yurakucho
Denki Bldg, 1-7-1 Yurakucho, Tokyo 100. (Club for foreign employees
of Japanese companies).
Foreign Executive Women (FEW), same address as above.
International Adventure Club, Tokyo British Club. Tel: (03) 327 2905.
Tokyo Leisure Club. Tel: (03) 3466 3925.
International Community Circle, 5F Shuwa Roppongi Bldg, 3-14-12
Roppongi, Minato-ku, Tokyo 106. Tel: (03) 3423 0660.

FOREIGN EMBASSIES IN TOKYO

Australian Embassy, 1-12 Shiba Koen 1-chome, Minato-ku, Tokyo 105.
Tel: (03) 3435 0971.
Canadian Embassy, 3-38 Akasaka 7-chome, Minato-ku, Tokyo 107.
Tel: (03) 3408 0971.
Embassy of New Zealand, 20-40 Kamiyacho, Shibuya-ka, Tokyo 150.
Tel: (03) 3467 2271.
Embassy of the United Kingdom, 1 Ichiban-cho, Chiyoda-ku, Tokyo 102.
Tel: (03) 3265 5511.
United States Embassy, 10-5 Akasaka 1-chome, Minato-ku, Tokyo 107.
Tel: (03) 3224 5000.

MAJOR BRANCHES OF THE MINISTRY OF JUSTICE IMMIGRATION BUREAU

Osaka: 31 Tanimachi 2-chome, Higashi-ku, Osaka.
Tel: (06) 941 0771.

Nagoya: 3-1 Sannomaru 4-chome, Naka-ku, Nagoya.
Tel: (052) 951 2391.

Sapporo: Odori-nishi 12-chome, Chuo-ku, Sapporo.
               Tel: (11) 261 9211.

Tokyo: 1-1 Kasumigaseki 1-chome, Chiyoda-ku Tokyo.
               Tel: (03) 3580 4111.

LOW COST TEMPORARY ACCOMMODATION IN JAPAN'S MAJOR CITIES

Tokyo
ABC House, Kamata. Tel: (03) 3736 2311.
Ajima House, Musashi Sakai. Tel: (03) 3331 4607.
Apple House, Waseda.   Tel: (03) 3232 7721.
              Kichijoji.   Tel: (03) 3870 2855.
Asia Center, Minato-ku, Akasaka 8-10-32. Tel: (03) 3402 6111.
Bilingual House (various locations). Tel: (03) 3200 7082.
Cosmopolitan Guest House. Tel: (03) 3926 4746.
Fantasy Villa Guest House. Tel: (03) 3334 6293.
Friendship Guest House (3 locations in Tokyo). Tel: (03) 3327 3179.
Fuji Guest House. Tel: (03) 3967 446.
Hoshino Mansions. Tel: (03) 3657 1425.
Ikebukuro House, Toshima-ku, Ikebukuro. Tel: (03) 3984 3399.
Ikenohata Bunka Center, Taito-ku, Ikenohata 1-3-45.
    Tel: (03) 3822 0151.
International Youth Hostel, Kaguragashi, Shinjuku-ku.
    Tel: (03) 3235 1107.
International Guest House, Ginza. Tel: (03) 3623 8445.
International House, Musashi Sakai. Tel: (03) 3326 4839.
Japan YMCA Hostel, 4-8-8 Kudan Minami, Chiyoda-ku.
    Tel: (03) 3264 0661.
Japan House (2 locations). Tel: (03) 3962 2495.
Kimi Ryokan, 2-36-8 Ikebukuro, Toshima-ku. Tel: (03) 3971 3766.
Maharajah Guest House. Tel: (03) 3748 568.
Marui House. Tel: (03) 3962 4979.
Mickey Guest House, Kami Itabashi. Tel: (03) 3936 88891.
Miracle House, Omori-machi. Tel: (03) 3761 8099.
Okayasu Ryokan, 1-7-11 Shibaura, Minato-ku. Tel: (03) 3452 5091.
Okubo Guest House, 1-11-32 Hyakunin-cho, Shinjuku-ku.
    Tel: (03) 3361 2348.
Otsuka Sun Hotel, 2-40-8 Minami-Otsuka, Toshima-ku.
    Tel: (03) 3944 1151.
Rikko Kaikan, 2-43-12 Kotake-cho, Narima-ku. Tel: (03) 3972 1151.
Ryokan Katsutaro, 4-16-8 Ikenohata, Taito-ku. Tel: (03) 3821 9808.

Sawanoya Ryokan, 2-3-11 Yanaka, Taito-ku. Tel: (03) 3822 2251.
Shin Nakano Lodge, 6-1-1 Honcho, Nakano-ku. Tel: (03) 3381 4886.
Tokyo YWCA, Higashi-Nakano. Tel: (03) 3940 4705.
Yoyogi Youth Hostel, 3-1 Kamizono-cho, Yoyogi, Shibuya-ku.
   Tel: (03) 3467 9163.
Tokyo House, Ogikubo.   Tel: (03) 3391 5577.
                Otsuka.   Tel: (03) 3910 8808.
Town House, Akabane, Ueno. Tel: (03) 3320 3201.
YMCA Asia Youth Center, 2-5-5 Sarugaku-cho, Chiyoda-ku.
   Tel: (03) 3233 0631.

Osaka

Gyokusenji Youth Hostel, 1438 Yamabe, Nose-cho, Toyono-ku.
   Tel: (0727) 34 0844.
Hattori Ryokuchi Youth Hostel, 1-3 Hattori Ryokuchi, Toyonaka-shi.
   Tel: (06) 862 0600.
Nagai Youth Hostel, Higashi Nagai-cho, Higashi Sumiyoshi-ku.
   Tel: (06) 699 5631.
Sayama Youth Hostel. Tel: (06) 699 5631.
Shoto Hotel, 5-9 Togano-cho, Kita-ku. Tel: (06) 312 9351.

Kobe

Kobe Gajoen Hotel, 8-4-23 Shimo Yamate dori, Chuo-ku.
   Tel: (078) 341 31.
Mudo-ji Youth Hostel. Tel: (078) 581 0250.
Tarumi Youth Hostel. Tel: (078) 707 2133.

Nagoya

Business Hotel Kiyoshi, 1-3-1 Heiwa, Naka-ku. Tel: (052) 321 5663.
Nagoya Green Hotel, Naka-ku. Tel: (052) 203 0211.
Nagoya Youth Hostel, 1-50 Kameira, Tashiro-cho, Chikusa-ku.
   Tel: (052) 781 9845.
Oyone Ryokan, 2-2-12 Aoi, Higashi-ku. Tel: (052) 936 8788.
Seinen Kaikan Youth Hostel. Tel: (052) 221 6001.

Kyoto

Tani Guest House, 3 Kisho-in-cho, Minami-ku. Tel: (075) 661 2391.
Higashiyama Youth Hostel, Shirakawabashi, Goken-cho, Sanjo Dori,
   Higashiyama-ku. Tel: (075) 761 8135.
Tani Guest House, 8 Murasakino, Daitokuji-cho, Kita-ku.
   Tel: (075) 492 5489.

Kaijusenji Youth Hostel. Tel: (075) 476 2256.

Kyoto Ohara Youth Hostel. Tel: (075) 744 2528.

Pension Shimogamo, 20 Kamikawaracho, Shimogamo, Sakyo-ku.
  Tel: (075) 711 0180.

Pension Koto, 132 Kuzekawaharacho, Minami-ku. Tel: (075) 934 5010.

Pension Higashiyama Gion, Sanjo Sagaru, Shirakawasuji, Higashiyama-
  ku. Tel: (075) 882 1181.

Utano Youth Hostel, Nakayama-cho, Uzumasa, Ukyo-ku.
  Tel: (075) 462 2288.

Yuhara Ryokan, 188 Kiyamachi-dori, Kagiya-cho, Shimogyo-ku.
  Tel: (075) 371 9583.

Index